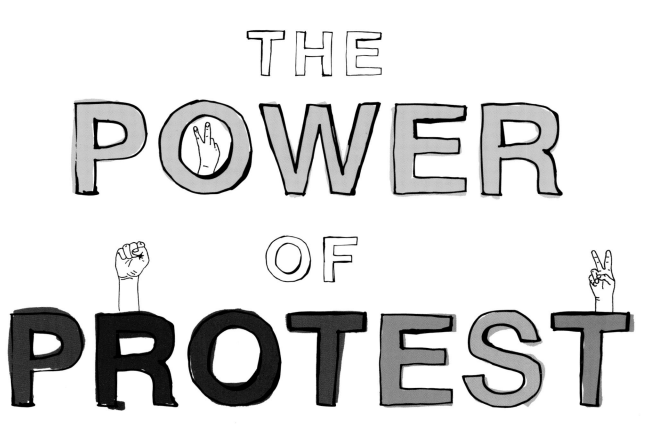

THE POWER OF PROTEST

A VISUAL HISTORY of the Moments That Changed the World

sourcebooks

TABLE OF CONTENTS

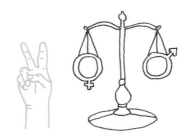

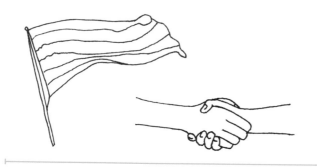

"

People say, what is the sense of our small effort? They cannot see that we must lay one brick at a time, take one step at a time. A pebble cast into a pond causes ripples that spread in all directions. Each one of our thoughts, words, and deeds is like that. No one has a right to sit down and feel hopeless. There is too much work to do.

—DOROTHY DAY

THE FIGHT FOR PEACE and FREEDOM

1961

The Berlin Wall is erected, dividing the city into East and West Germany.

1969

More than 2 million Americans participate in the antiwar Moratorium Day.

1970

Students protesting the bombing of Cambodia are fired upon at Kent State University in Ohio.

1869

First Laulupidu, or Song Festival, occurs during Estonia's Great Awakening.

"mu isamaa, mu õnn ja rõõm"

1930

Gandhi begins his Salt March across western India.

1968

Riots break loose at the Democratic National Convention in Chicago.

1971

New York Times publishes the Pentagon Papers.

1970

President Richard Nixon announces expansion of the Vietnam War into Cambodia.

1988

A singing protest against Soviet domination is held at a pop music festival in Tartu, Estonia.

1989

The Berlin Wall falls.

2003–2005

Color Revolutions occur in Soviet Republics.

2011

Tens of thousands all over Egypt protest against the rule of Hosni Mubarak, forcing him to resign.

1975

North Vietnamese Army captures Saigon, South Vietnam's capital, marking the end of the war.

1989

As many as 100,000 Chinese students march to Tiananmen Square on the day of Hu Yaobang's funeral.

1991

Estonia achieves independence.

2009

Protests break out in Iran when the reelection of Mahmoud Ahmadinejad is announced; millions demonstrate in Tehran.

2014

General Abdel Fattah al-Sisi, who led the army coup that removed President Mohamed Morsi from power, becomes Egypt's next elected president.

2013

Activist Ahmed Maher, a prominent participant in the Tahrir Square protests, is arrested and sentenced to three years in prison.

CEASE-FIRE!
All GIs Out of Viet in 60 Days

TOP: **Mohandas K. Gandhi, early 1940s.**
BOTTOM: **Poet and Satyagraha leader Sarojini Naidu, 1946.**
LEFT: **Gandhi walking the shoreline during the Salt March.**

GANDHI'S SALT MARCH

" "

Each time a man stands up for an ideal, or acts to improve the lot of others, or strikes out against injustice, he sends forth a tiny ripple of hope.

—ROBERT F. KENNEDY

IN THE SPRING of 1930, the Salt March opened a campaign of civil disobedience in India aimed at ending British rule on the subcontinent. The protest action, also known as the Dandi March and the Salt Satyagraha, was led by a man who had begun advocating for Indian independence while practicing law in England. Returning to India, Mohandas K. Gandhi, who soon would be revered as the Mahatma (or great-souled being), developed a strategy that relied on peaceful civil disobedience, or *satyagraha* ("insistence on truth," a term Gandhi coined based on Sanskrit roots).

Salt was an essential substance to Indians, because it served not only as seasoning but as a preservative for food in a country where only the wealthy could afford refrigeration. However, the British monopolized the production and distribution of salt and would not allow the Indians to sell it. Moreover, the Indians, most of whom were very poor, had to buy their salt, heavily taxed and at inflated prices, from the British. Indians had been protesting the salt tax since the nineteenth century. In 1930, led by Gandhi, they would protest it effectively.

The Salt March began on March 12, 1930, near Gandhi's ashram in the vicinity of Ahmadabad in western India. A few dozen followers accompanied their leader, stopping at a different village each night, where Gandhi would rally the locals to the cause. On April 5, hundreds of marchers reached their destination, the little town of Dandi, near Surat, on the coast of the Arabian Sea, some 240 miles from Ahmadabad. The next day, the people committed their first act of *satyagraha*: they picked up handfuls of salt deposits, thus disobeying the law against "producing" the mineral. No one was arrested.

However, over the next two months, thousands of Indians picked up salt and were arrested and jailed. In May, Gandhi himself was arrested, an event that inspired tens of thousands of others to join the *satyagraha*. Led now by the poet Sarojini Naidu, the marchers persisted despite beatings by the police.

With 60,000 people straining the capacity of area prisons, the British decided to negotiate, releasing Gandhi so that he could treat with Lord Irwin, the viceroy, who was King George V's representative in India. A truce was declared and signed on March 5, 1931, nearly a year after the beginning of the *satyagraha*. As a result, the imprisoned protesters were released and Indians were allowed to produce salt for domestic use.

Protesters used the *satyagraha* repeatedly in the decades-long quest for Indian independence, which was finally achieved in 1947. Gandhi died in 1948. Peace and freedom seekers the world over have adopted his technique of civil disobedience. In the United States, Dr. Martin Luther King Jr. was one of its foremost practitioners. ■

TOP: **Crowd and Gandhi on the Salt March.**

"" ""

Power is of two kinds. One is obtained by the fear of punishment and the other by acts of love. Power based on love is a thousand times more effective and permanent than the one derived from fear of punishment.

—MOHANDAS K. GANDHI

DEMOCRATIC NATIONAL
CONVENTION RIOTS

" "

Our position is that whoever the candidates are, and whatever the platforms, that we must stay in the streets and stay in active resistance or else there will be no peace. Either in the ghettos or in Vietnam.

—DAVE DELLINGER

TOP: **A student protester eyes riot police outside the national convention.**
BOTTOM: **Demonstrators attack police officers during a clash.**
LEFT: **Students crowd the General Logan Monument in Grant Park, Chicago, in protest.**

THE RIOTS IN Chicago in August 1968 lie at the opposite end of the spectrum from the *satyagraha*-based protests of India and the peaceful civil disobedience actions of American civil rights workers in the 1950s and 1960s.

Leading up to the convention, Democratic Party leaders who were preparing to meet in Chicago to nominate their presidential ticket for the November election were apprehensive, knowing that thousands of young opponents of the war in Vietnam had planned a protest to coincide with the party's national convention. As events unfolded, protest actions that at first were merely disruptive turned violent. The Chicago police, who later shouldered much of the blame for the violence, had been ready for trouble.

Mayor Richard J. Daley had assured leaders of the Democratic Party, who had wanted to move the convention to Miami, that the Windy City would be peaceful and no outrageous demonstrations would be permitted. To discourage the Democrats from

PORTRAITS OF THE CHICAGO SEVEN, LEFT TO RIGHT: **Jerry Rubin, Abbie Hoffman, Tom Hayden, David Dellinger, John Froines, Lee Weiner, Rennie Davis.**

backing out, he threatened to withdraw his support from the party's assumed nominee, Hubert Humphrey. Daley also had the entrance to the venue, the International Amphitheatre, bulletproofed and surrounded with a steel fence topped with barbed wire. The Democrats agreed to stay.

Plans for an antiwar protest coinciding with the Chicago convention had been in the works since March, when activists met at a camp some twenty-five miles northwest of the city to coordinate events. The leaders included *Liberation* magazine editor and chairman of the National Mobilization Committee to End War in Vietnam (Mobe), David Dellinger;

Rennie Davis, project director for Mobe; and Tom Hayden, one of the founders of Students for a Democratic Society (SDS). Also present were Abbie Hoffman and Jerry Rubin of the Youth International Party (the YIPPIES).

While the protest organizers were meeting, President Lyndon B. Johnson announced his decision not to run for reelection. His approval ratings were below 30 percent, and his war policies were even less popular. This news might have derailed the activists' plans, but when it was announced that Vice President Humphrey would seek the nomination, the protest was back on track. Humphrey was closely identified

with Johnson, and many in the antiwar movement wanted to support Senator Robert Kennedy or one of his Senate colleagues, Eugene McCarthy or George McGovern.

Tensions were compounded in April by the assassination of Dr. Martin Luther King Jr. and the accompanying riots. In short order, protests organized by SDS virtually shut down Columbia University. On June 5, Robert Kennedy was shot in the head right after his victory in the California primary. He died the next day, and young people all over the country concluded that they had to go to Chicago.

By the day of the Democratic National Convention in Chicago,

inside the convention center, with its periodically nonfunctioning air conditioning, the so-called peace plank delegates made it clear to television audiences that Humphrey was not everyone's favorite. Screaming matches lasted into the early morning hours, but Humphrey was nominated nevertheless, and chose Maine senator Edmund Muskie as his running mate.

Between August 23 and 29, the antiwar demonstrators camped in parks or in spaces volunteered by churches, businesses, and private individuals. Rennie Davis spoke of "a new constituency for America...a new urgency, and a new approach." Fired

up by speeches and a picnic two days before the convention opened, but without a precise plan, the protesters marched on the convention center on August 26, only to encounter thousands of Chicago police officers, Army and Illinois National Guard troops, and Secret Service agents.

Chicago policemen, having removed their badges, used batons and billy clubs to beat protesters to the ground. Reporters, doctors, and bystanders who attempted to help the wounded were beaten as well. The close-packed crowd was teargassed. When the protests ended on August 29, the report from the city's police cited 589 arrests, with

119 police officers and 100 protesters injured. A government-funded report put most of the blame for the violence on the police; Mayor Daley reacted by giving them a raise.

The following spring, a grand jury in Chicago indicted eight police officers and eight civilians to answer charges in connection with the riots. The protesters who appeared were Mobe, SDS, and YIPPIE leaders as well two academics and a founder of the Black Panther Party. They were charged with violation of the Civil Rights Act of 1968, which declared "inciting to riot" a federal crime.

The defendants, defiant throughout, turned the trial into a circus; their attorneys repeatedly accused the judge of bias. The Black Panthers' Bobby Seale, after repeated outbursts that included direct insults to the judge, was gagged and chained to his chair. The judge declared a mistrial and sentenced Seale separately, apart from the other seven men on trial. Hence the phrase famous today is "the Chicago Seven."

The seven, plus two of their most outspoken attorneys, were convicted of contempt of court. The two academics were acquitted, but Dellinger, Davis, Hayden, Hoffman, and Rubin were fined $5,000 apiece, plus court costs, and sentenced to five years in prison. In 1970, the decisions were reversed on appeal, based on the trial judge's refusal to allow defense attorneys to screen prospective jurors for cultural and racial bias. The contempt charges were retried, and a different judge found Dellinger, Rubin, Hoffman, and William Kunstler, one of the attorneys, guilty of some charges; no fines or sentences were imposed.

However, protests against the war in Vietnam continued, as did demonstrations for civil rights causes

and civil unrest culminating in riots in many U.S. cities.

The Democrats, who had elected Johnson in 1964 with 61.1 percent of the popular vote, were scarred by Humphrey's loss to Richard Nixon. The presence of third-party candidates in 1968 had contributed to that result, but the next Democratic president, Jimmy Carter, served only one term, and electoral success for the party in the years since then has been intermittent. ■

TOP: **The Chicago Seven and their attorneys raise fists outside the court.**
RIGHT: **A Chicago officer carries a child who fainted during demonstrations.**

"THE CONFRONTATION WAS NOT CREATED BY THE POLICE; THE CONFRONTATION WAS CREATED BY THE PEOPLE WHO CHARGED THE POLICE. GENTLEMEN, LET'S GET THE THING STRAIGHT, ONCE AND FOR ALL. THE POLICEMAN ISN'T THERE TO CREATE DISORDER; THE POLICEMAN IS THERE TO PRESERVE DISORDER."

—RICHARD J. DALEY

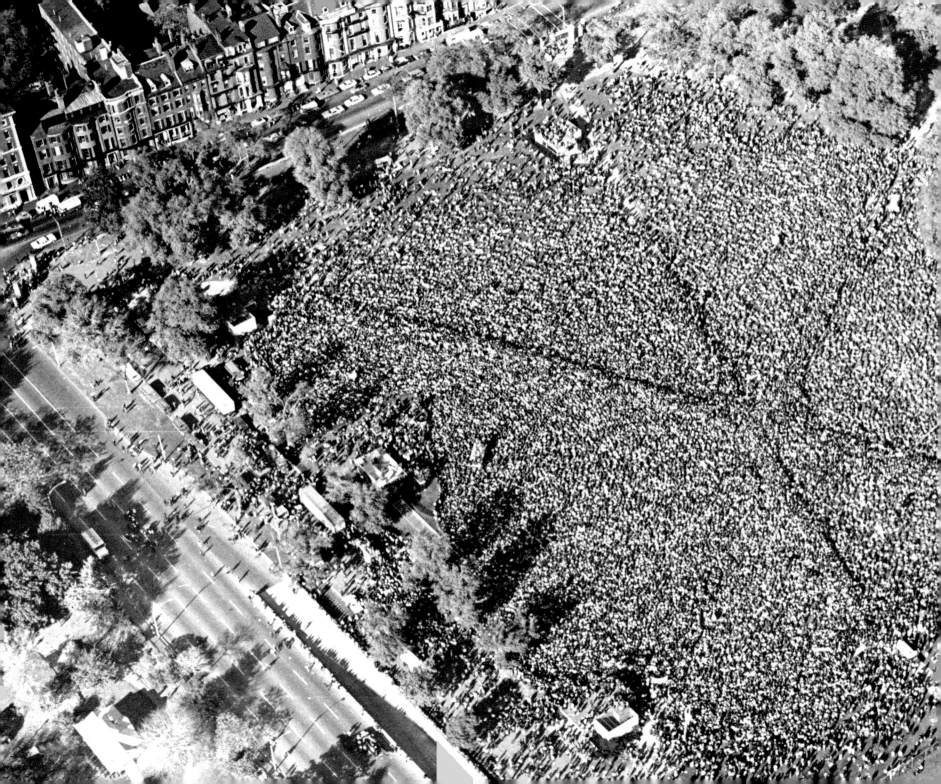

MORATORIUM MOVEMENT
TO END THE WAR IN VIETNAM

" "

When the rich wage war, it is the poor who die.

—JEAN-PAUL SARTRE

TOP: **A pin advertising the moratorium rally in Washington.**
BOTTOM: **Paul Stookey and Peter Yarrow of the group Peter, Paul, and Mary perform from the podium at the moratorium.**
LEFT: **A large crowd gathers in the Boston Common for the moratorium.**

THE EVENT BELIEVED to be the largest antiwar protest in U.S. history was a rally held in Washington, DC, on November 15, 1969. The crowd, numbering as many as 500,000 people, was double the number of participants in the 1963 March on Washington for Peace and Freedom. Many committed activists marched on both occasions, evidence of a rising concern about these fundamental issues among Americans. That concern was shared by participants in smaller marches all over the country.

Staged by a coalition group, the Vietnam Moratorium Committee, the program included speeches by antiwar politicians and music by Peter, Paul, and Mary and Arlo Guthrie; the crowd, led by Pete Seeger, sang "Give Peace a Chance." A description of the crowd in the *New York Times* depicts a "predominantly youthful" group incorporating "the moderate and radical left...old-style liberals; Communists and pacifists and a sprinkling of the violent New Left." To make sure things didn't get out of hand, the committee fielded

3,000 "march marshals" to watch for signs of trouble, who were given permission to intervene as necessary.

Opposition to the Vietnam War had been building since the recently ended Johnson administration, with college students and many of their instructors in the forefront. Thus on October 15, exactly a month before the Washington rally, more than 2 million Americans called a halt: they set aside all non-peace-related activities, including school and work, to participate in public demonstrations and to attend teach-ins, rallies, and candlelight vigils, all to draw public attention to reasons for stopping the war. In Boston, the largest protest attracted 100,000 people, who heard speeches by distinguished professors and articulate students from the city's colleges and universities.

The day after the first moratorium, a group called the Resistance collected more than 1,000 draft cards, which they later delivered to the Department of Justice in Washington. This was a deliberate act of civil disobedience, since most of the protesters had student deferments, secured precisely so that they wouldn't be drafted. By relinquishing this protection, they were setting themselves up to be prosecuted for defying the selective service laws then in effect. The strategic goal was to overload the federal courts with draft cases, leading the Nixon administration to end the war quickly. In hindsight, this seems naive, but the young men in the Resistance saw their act as one of moral witness.

President Nixon's public reaction to the second moratorium in November 1969 was dismissive impatience. He advised the press that he had enough to do running the country and did not intend to undertake running the colleges and universities. He concluded by remarking that although "this kind of activity" was to be expected, the rally wouldn't affect his policy making. The recollections of senior members of his administration, published years later, suggest that the truth was more complicated.

LEFT: **Protesters holding signs at the moratorium.**
RIGHT: **Coretta Scott King leading a march as part of the moratorium.**

The Power of Protest

The impact of the moratorium movement was debated throughout the remainder of the twentieth century. Initial evaluations by former activists credited their movement with having ended the war. The first historians to write about it, lacking information revealed later, tended to reach the same conclusion.

However, some later analysts have concluded that the protests helped prolong the war. This view is usually advanced by those who believe that the United States could have won in Vietnam if the war were more supported in the United States. These writers had the advantage of memoirs and historical accounts by high officials in the Johnson and Nixon administrations, as well as official documents declassified in 1975, after the end of the war. (The United States had ended direct involvement in the conflict in 1973.)

At the time of the first moratorium in October 1969, Nixon's cabinet had been putting the final touches on Operation Duck Hook, an escalation program that included land invasion of North Vietnam, bombing dikes to destroy food supplies, and saturation bombing of Hanoi and Haiphong; the nuclear option also had been discussed. On November 1, 1969, Nixon decided to abandon Duck Hook. His secretary of defense, Melvin Laird, later referred to the "tremendous influence" the recent protest had exerted.

Both Johnson and Nixon weighed geopolitical considerations involving the Soviet Union and China, as well as the influence (actual and potential) of the protests. Much perceptive analysis of geopolitical data was available to the civilian population in articles in specialized journals like *Foreign Affairs* magazine and in think-tank reports, which were read by few outsiders. But even the 1971 publication of the Pentagon Papers in the *New York Times* did not seem to hasten the end of hostilities.

Opinion remains divided as to whether the antiwar protests prolonged the war or helped bring it to an end. The protesters themselves, some of whom went on to teach in prestigious

colleges and universities, remain persuaded that they had met a moral obligation by working to end the killing. They dismiss the charge that the killing might have stopped much earlier if U.S. policy makers had not refrained, out of concern for public opinion, from ending the war via dramatic escalation.

Attempting to model alternative outcomes of a historical situation on the basis of possibilities that can't be known or anticipated with certainty is notoriously difficult. Thus it's certain that discussion of U.S. involvement in Vietnam, memorably described as a quagmire, will continue. ■

KENT STATE RIOTS

“ ”

My God! My God! They're killing us!

—KENT STATE FRESHMAN RON STEELE

TOP: **Masked Guardsmen teargas
Kent State students.**
BOTTOM: **Flag-waving student protester jumps
over blood spilled by one of the students shot.**
LEFT: **Students hurl tear gas back
at the National Guardsmen.**

MEMBERS OF THE Ohio National Guard discharged sixty-seven rounds in thirteen seconds into a crowd one morning in May 1970 in Kent, Ohio. They were under orders to disperse some 2,000 people, many of them students at Kent State University, who were protesting the expansion of the Vietnam War into Cambodia. The casualties rocked the nation: four dead and nine wounded, one of whom was permanently paralyzed.

The United States had been participating in the long-running war between the northern and southern parts of Vietnam since 1961. Commitments of troops and money had been on a small scale until 1964. Popular opposition began in earnest in 1965, when deaths in Vietnam increased to 1,928, from 216 in the preceding year. The moratoriums of 1968 and 1969 drew even more people, mainly students, into the antiwar camp. Although the death toll had dropped by April 30, 1970, when President Richard Nixon announced U.S. military action in Cambodia, the public responded with nationwide protests, including a student strike in which 4 million participated.

At Kent State, the May 1, 1970, protests were angry rather than peaceful. A copy of the Constitution was burned, and after midnight, off campus, students joined bar patrons, bikers, and homeless people in rowdiness that ended when police used tear gas. The next day, Ohio governor Jim Rhodes granted the city's request for National Guard troops, amid rumors that "a significant proportion" of the rioters weren't Kent State students. Tear gas was used again that night, and some students were arrested for curfew violation.

On Sunday, May 3, Governor Rhodes floridly blamed outside agitators, calling them "worse than the Brown Shirts and the Communist element." Students left campus to assist with cleanup in the town, but that night there was another rally at the school, which Guardsmen dispersed with tear gas. Students participating in the subsequent sit-in elsewhere on campus were forced back to their dorms, some at the point of bayonets.

The widely publicized campus protest scheduled for May 4 attracted nearly 2,000 people, not all of them students. When the speeches started, the Guard attempted to disperse the crowd, which first threw rocks and then returned airborne tear gas canisters to the troops. In retrospect, the Guard seems not to have planned for all contingencies.

The shooting reportedly started at 12:24 p.m., at which time the Guardsmen appeared to have been trapped between the protesters and a chain-link fence. The details of the thirteen-second fusillade, as well as the Guardsmen's reason for opening fire, remain obscure; a presidential commission later criticized both sides but called the shootings "unnecessary, unwarranted, and inexcusable." Forensic investigation disclosed that fifty-five of the sixty-seven rounds had been fired into the air and into the ground. Two of the students killed had been participating in the protest; the others had been walking from one class to another. While the Kent State protest had disastrous consequences, shedding light on government overreach and police brutality, the protesters demonstrated not only the ferocity of antiwar sentiment but also their bravery and resilience in the face of multiple attempts at repression. ∎

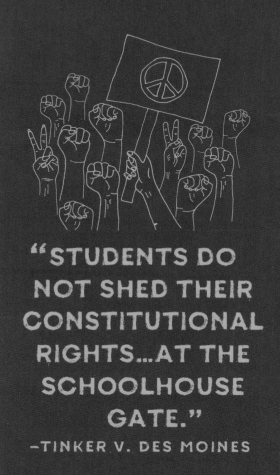

"STUDENTS DO NOT SHED THEIR CONSTITUTIONAL RIGHTS...AT THE SCHOOLHOUSE GATE."
—TINKER V. DES MOINES

MUHARRAM
PROTESTS

" "

Noble people of Iran! Press forward with your movement and do not slacken for a minute, as I know full well you will not!

—IMAM KHOMEINI

TOP: **Demonstrators march on Ashura Day in Tehran, 1978.**

THE SHORT-LIVED (1925–1979) Pahlavi dynasty never enjoyed universal popularity in Iran. Reza Shah Pahlavi, the founder, was a former military officer whose coup d'état in 1921 led to the deposition of Ahmad Shah Qajar, the last of the centuries-old Qajar dynasty. Reza Shah introduced westernizing reforms, including the encouragement of women to be active outside the home, which met with the approval of the middle and upper classes. The Muslim clergy and many of their followers, as well as the tribal people the rulers scorned, opposed these reforms. The first Pahlavi shah wanted to maintain neutrality during World War II, but this did not sit well with Britain, which owned the Anglo-Iranian Oil Company.

Reza Shah abdicated in 1941, when the Allies invaded and occupied Iran, prompting the surrender of fifteen military divisions. However, the British allowed the ruler to save face by agreeing to turn over the reins to one of his sons, Crown Prince Mohammad Reza.

The second shah soon clashed with

> **"It was a revolution that took everyone by surprise—even the Iranians."**
>
> —LIZ THURGOOD

a parliament-named prime minister, Mohammad Mossadegh, who had nationalized the country's oil industry, thus ending Britain's role in the company formerly known as Anglo-Iranian Oil. Fearing dire consequences, Mohammad Reza fled into exile. Two years later, in 1953, a coup ousted Mossadegh, who was then arrested by army officers who favored the Pahlavis.

Back in power, the shah put in motion plans for the country that produced a booming economy, a new middle class, and a military that was once again respected in the Middle East. Alongside the army was the new Organization of Intelligence and National Security (SAVAK), part secret police, part homeland security service, and part intelligence agency. Among the factors driving Iran's 1979 revolution was hatred of SAVAK, which ruthlessly pursued, arrested, tortured, and executed regime opponents.

Always ambitious for himself and for his country, the second Reza Shah saw Iran, home of the ancient Persian culture, as superior to some of its neighbors on the Arabian Peninsula: the countries with large tribal populations of uneducated, nomadic people who avoided both the cities and the oil industry. But the shah's overall plan, styled the White Revolution because it was to be bloodless, was opposed by the powerful Islamic clergy. The mullahs also demanded the return of Shiite grand ayatollah Ruhollah Khomeini, who had denounced the shah in 1964 and had later been exiled.

On December 2, 1979 (year 1408 in the Islamic calendar), Iranians were approaching a hinge point in their national life—the overthrow of the Pahlavi dynasty. In consultation with Khomeini, then living outside Paris, opponents of the shah had planned a series of protests during the holy month of Muharram. Aware of the

coming demonstrations, the shah had his allies in the military ban street demonstrations and extend the curfew.

Participants in the first protest, over 2 million strong, flooded Tehran's Shahyad Square. Many were teens recruited by mullahs. To emphasize their religious ardor, youthful protesters visibly broke the curfew by going out at night and shouting *"Allahu Akbar!"* from the rooftops. The atmosphere struck some observers as benign, almost like a holiday, with a minimum of manhandling of protesters. However, the government said that at least twelve had died.

The demands were the same in protests all over the country: the shah was to leave power and the grand ayatollah was to be allowed back in the country. On December 10 and 11, the protest extended to cities all over Iran, for a total number of Muharram demonstrators in the millions.

Those marches too were peaceful.

RIGHT: **Anti-shah demonstrators marching through Tehran.**

Ayatollah Shariatmadari had negotiated an agreement with the shah in which the cleric guaranteed a nonviolent protest in exchange for the release of political prisoners, including Karim Sanjabi, the leader of the anti-shah National Front. The deal necessarily included an end to the ban on street demonstrations. A coalition of mullahs and local merchants ensured that anyone who became aggressive was prevented from causing harm.

Crowd estimates for all the Muharram marches range between 6 million and 9 million, roughly 10 percent of Iran's population. For purposes of comparison, revolutionary protesters in eighteenth-century France, early twentieth-century Russia, and Romania in 1989 have been calculated, with varying confidence limits, at around 1 percent each.

Khomeini returned to Iran on February 1, 1979. The shah and his family had left the country some two weeks earlier. ■

SINGING
REVOLUTION

"Mu isamaa, mu õnn ja rõõm"

" "

A nation who makes its revolution by singing and smiling should be a sublime example to all.

—HEINZ VALK

THE PEOPLE OF Estonia, the northernmost of the Baltic countries, have a 6,000-year history of living both independently and in subjugation to other European states. Around the time of the American Civil War, with the descendants of earlier German conquerors in control, the descendants of the original Estonians began to work toward self-rule.

In 1869, the movement called the Great Awakening gave birth to the national song festival, Laulupidu. In the turmoil of World War I, Estonian nationalists declared and lost independence, fighting first the forces of imperial Germany and then the Russian Bolsheviks. In 1920, Soviet Russia recognized Estonia's independence. World War II changed all that: the Soviets reneged on prior agreements and resumed control over Estonia as well as Latvia and Lithuania.

During the early years of Soviet occupation, Estonia lost roughly a quarter of its population: some were executed, others imprisoned or deported; still others escaped. Few felt like singing. In 1947, the first Laulupidu held under the Soviets featured a patriotic song, "Land of My Fathers, Land That I Love." The anthem was banned in the 1950s, but Estonians sang it anyway. By 1965, it was back on the song festival program. In 1969, on the 100th anniversary of the song festival, the audience sang along with the performers on stage. Soviet authorities ordered the choirs to leave the stage, but no one moved. A large Soviet military band was ordered to play, but more than 100,000 Estonians easily drowned it out.

Fifteen years passed, and a half-dozen rock songs temporarily replaced "Land of My Fathers" as live music at large public gatherings. The Estonians were on thin ice here, but took the chance that the Soviets would not dispatch tanks against nonviolent protest activities. Emboldened, the people launched a series of mass gatherings to sing patriotic songs.

The first large-scale singing protest in this cycle occurred at a pop music festival in Tartu, Estonia's second-largest city, in 1988. The next year, the official part of the Old Town Festival in the capital, Tallinn, was followed by the singing of patriotic songs at the city's Song Festival Grounds. Later that summer, artists performing at the Summer Rock Festival also sang patriotic songs. In September, more than a quarter-million people (more than 25 percent of the country's population) came to the Song of Estonia festival in Tallinn. For the first time, Estonian leaders and ordinary citizens publicly gave spoken expression to their desire for independence.

The Singing Revolution continued until 1991, when the Estonian legislature, together with the Estonian Supreme Soviet, opposed Moscow by announcing the restoration of the independent state of Estonia. The announcement on August 20 did provoke the Soviets into sending tanks. However, the next day, people acting as human shields faced down the armored vehicles that advanced on Tallinn; Estonia had achieved independence. ■

"A VOICE IS A HUMAN GIFT; IT SHOULD BE CHERISHED AND USED, TO UTTER FULLY HUMAN SPEECH AS POSSIBLE. POWERLESSNESS AND SILENCE GO TOGETHER."
—MARGARET ATWOOD

BERLIN WALL
PROTESTS

" "

On October 9, 1989...the people of Leipzig showed us what citizens can achieve when they believe in their own strength and take their destiny into their own hands.

—HORST KOEHLER

TOP: **Graffiti painted on one of the preserved Berlin Wall sections at the East Side Gallery, 1990.**
BOTTOM: **John F. Kennedy visiting the Berlin Wall at Checkpoint Charlie, 1963.**

"TWO THOUSAND YEARS ago, the proudest boast was *'Civis romanus sum'* [I am a Roman citizen]. Today, in the world of freedom, the proudest boast is *'Ich bin ein Berliner!'*... All free men, wherever they may live, are citizens of Berlin, and therefore, as a free man, I take pride in the words *'Ich bin ein Berliner.'"*

John F. Kennedy spoke those words from the steps of the Rathaus, or city hall, of the state senate of Tempelhof-Schöneberg in West Berlin on June 26, 1963, two years after the erection of the Berlin Wall and sixteen years before its demolition.

East German authorities had built the heavily fortified and guarded wall to slow to a trickle the 3.5-million-strong flood of East Germans who had escaped the poverty, drudgery, and oppression of the German Democratic Republic (GDR). Soviet leader Joseph Stalin had urged leaders of the GDR to improve their border offenses in 1952, but infrastructural considerations prevented the puppet officials from completing the job until the dictator had been dead for almost a decade.

The tense Cold War brought East

Germans years of misery that drifted into hopelessness. However, one church in the southeastern Saxon city of Leipzig gave rise to a series of peaceful demonstrations that were instrumental in bringing about the fall of the Berlin Wall. These were the Monday Demonstrations, which began on September 4, 1989, after the weekly prayer for peace at the St. Nicholas Church. That first spontaneous demonstration by a few hundred people struck a chord, and soon participants filled not only the church but the nearby Karl Marx Square (since restored to its original name, Augustenplatz).

Because they understood they had the support of the Lutheran Church, people came to the demonstrations to make demands for democratic reforms and to secure freedom of travel. Throughout the GDR, Germans learned of the protests from friends in West Germany and held their own events in their own city squares on Monday evenings. By October 9, more than 70,000 Leipzig residents were in the streets chanting *"Wir sind das Volk!"* (We are the people!).

Meanwhile, the GDR government was collapsing, as increasing numbers of East Germans were leaving, thanks to recent relaxations in the hated travel restrictions. Longtime Socialist Unity Party boss Erich Honecker resigned on October 18, just two days after a Monday Demonstration by 320,000 people. Growing popular dissatisfaction, as well as uncertainty in the ranks of GDR leadership, led to the fall of the Berlin Wall on November 9.

The protests continued as peaceful reminders of the people's will until March 1990, when free elections were held in the GDR, an important step. ■

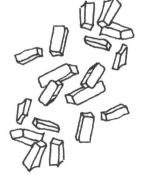

LEFT: **Crowd celebrating the fall of the Berlin Wall, 1989.**

TIANANMEN SQUARE

" "

We, the Tiananmen generation, are young enough and stubborn enough to keep speaking out until the world is also on our side.

—WU'ER KAIXI

THE SCENE OF the Tiananmen Square massacre of 1989 lies in central Beijing. The Tiananmen itself, the Gate of Heavenly Peace, was the formal entryway to the Forbidden City: the royal residence, ceremonial venue, and political center of China for nearly 500 years. Today's Tiananmen Square, with the gate at its north end, was completed in 1959, in accordance with the wishes of Mao Zedong.

Mao died in 1976, and the country he had effectively ruled since 1949 struggled to adapt to the inevitable changes. Popular dissatisfaction emerged in many areas, including economic difficulties and the continued exclusion of most Chinese citizens from positions of authority in the ruling Communist Party.

In the mid-1980s, with reforms slow in coming, students took the lead in the quest for change. Inspired by Fang Lizhi, an astrophysicist just returned from a tenured professorship at Princeton, young people began to rally for a state that was both democratic and more accountable to the people than the

ABOVE: **Protester Wang Dan addresses students at the Square.**

ABOVE: **A student leads anti-government chants outside a pro-government rally in Beijing.**

government of Mao's successor, Deng Xiaoping; they also desired free speech and a free press. It was a tall order, which the government at first tried to ignore.

In 1987, when protests had spread from Hefei, where Fang lived, to Beijing, Shanghai, and other cities, Deng forced the resignation of the party's general secretary, Hu Yaobang, on grounds of being soft on protesters. The party then took stronger measures against the protesters. Hu's death in 1989, from a heart attack, seemed to trigger the events that culminated in the June massacre.

After two days during which unexpectedly large crowds went to the Square to mourn Hu, thousands of students representing different groups assembled there; within hours the gathering had become a protest, complete with a wish list that became known as the Seven Demands. It's unlikely that the protesters expected compliance with any of the demands, but the list did express their longing for freedom and democracy and their disgust with a corrupt government staffed by rent-seeking officials who declined to reveal their incomes.

Protests continued, and rioting broke out on the day of Hu's state funeral; a march to the Square of between 50 to 100,000 students on April 27 was supported by many outside the university community. The government was divided between hardliners who wanted to restore stability and a more reform-oriented faction who believed that the party should at least seem to support democratic values.

When there was eventually an agreement between these government parties to take steps toward dialogue

ABOVE: **"Tank Man" blocks a line of advancing tanks in Tiananmen Square.**

ABOVE: **A group of students sing in protest during one demonstration at the Square.**

with the students, the students responded by planning a hunger strike in the Square to coincide with a state visit by USSR president Mikhail Gorbachev. The *New York Times* reported that 150,000 students and others crowded the Square on the day of Gorbachev's arrival. During the visit, that number increased by hundreds of thousands, as people poured into the Square to support the hunger strikers. The disruption embarrassed eighty-four-year-old Deng in front of his much younger Soviet guest.

When Chinese party leaders subsequently met to discuss the escalating situation, the general secretary, Zhao Ziyang, advised making concessions to the students. Deng, who bore primary responsibility, declared martial law on May 20. The first wave of army troops, which arrived soon after, faced tens of thousands of demonstrators who blocked their vehicles, gave them food and water, and tried to persuade them to join the cause of democracy. Those troops withdrew on May 24, while leaders of the People's Liberation Army (PLA) planned a major mobilization.

On June 3, as evidence of the government's intent mounted, protesters caused some troops to retreat, but the afternoon brought ominous news: the move to "quell the counterrevolutionary riot" would begin that night. Troops were empowered to act in self-defense and to "use any means" to clear the Square.

Firing began in the neighboring area at 10:00 p.m.; shortly after midnight, a tank appeared in the Square and was soon joined by others. When students reacted with violence, endangering the lives of some troops, their leaders urged peaceful self-defense and confiscated rocks, bottles, and other makeshift weapons. As military reinforcements continued to arrive, two nonstudent demonstrators rode in an ambulance to speak to a PLA political commissar, who agreed to grant the students safe passage if they left the Square.

The news of the negotiation surprised many students, but by then, 4:30 a.m. on June 4, troops were advancing on them. Some who attempted to leave were beaten with clubs; others linked arms and marched out. The remainder refused to leave until they were beaten.

On June 5, a column of tanks exiting the Square was confronted by a man who moved to face them again when they tried to go around him. He then climbed onto the turret of one tank, spoke to the men inside, climbed down, and returned to his position. The demonstrator, known only as Tank Man, was pulled out of the way by onlookers.

On June 9, Deng spoke publicly to the army, praising the "martyrs" (some two dozen PLA soldiers and armed policemen were said to have died) and 7,000 comrades who were reportedly wounded.

Death tolls can't be ascertained reliably, given discrepancies between government and press statistics and the accumulated reports of participants. Western estimates put the total of civilian deaths between 400 and close to 1,000. A more extreme number, taken from a declassified British cable, estimates the death toll at 10,000. ∎

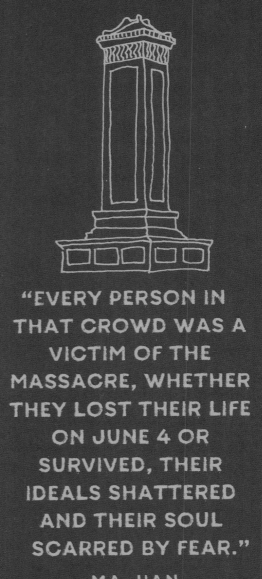

"EVERY PERSON IN THAT CROWD WAS A VICTIM OF THE MASSACRE, WHETHER THEY LOST THEIR LIFE ON JUNE 4 OR SURVIVED, THEIR IDEALS SHATTERED AND THEIR SOUL SCARRED BY FEAR."

–MA JIAN

TOP: **Fireworks above Independence Square in Kiev celebrating the election of Viktor Yushchenko (Orange Revolution), 2004.**

COLOR REVOLUTIONS

" "

The soul becomes dyed with the color of its thoughts.
—MARCUS AURELIUS

"COLOR REVOLUTION" IS the media's tag for a popular attempt to dispute an election or overthrow an oppressive or corrupt government. Most such movements are identified with a color— Rose, Green, Orange, or Pink. Some names represent another identifying word: Velvet for Czechoslovakia, Bulldozer for Yugoslavia. As a rule, the revolutionaries are nonviolent; regime reaction seldom is.

The peaceful twenty-day Rose Revolution in Georgia was the final step in the country's separation from Russia. In 1991, at the time of the collapse of the Soviet Union, Georgia had declared its independence, but the new government was unsuccessful. Eduard Shevardnadze, who took over in 1992, was an ineffective, unpopular leader. His resignation as head of the ruling party, the Citizens' Union of Georgia (CUG), did little to stem the tide of defections, and in local elections in 2002 the CUG was substantially outvoted. By then, mounting unrest in Georgia, stemming from internal conflicts and mistrust of Shevardnadze, had caused reductions in foreign aid.

However, nongovernmental

ABOVE: **Georgian protesters celebrate the resignation of Eduard Shevardnadze (Rose Revolution), 2003.**

ABOVE: **Crowds celebrate in Bishkek, Kyrgyzstan, on the anniversary of the Tulip Revolution, 2006.**

organizations often received funds from abroad, and homegrown groups as well as the U.S. Agency for International Development and George Soros's Open Society Institute supported the attempt by pro-Western Georgians to rid themselves of the corrupt, pro-Moscow Shevardnadze regime. Thus, the nationwide parliamentary elections on November 2, 2003, were closely monitored by accredited international organizations. Findings of procedural shortcomings came as no surprise, and by the middle of the month, organized acts of civil resistance were occurring throughout the country.

Important participants in the resistance were supporters of former Minister of Justice Mikheil Saakashvili, the United National Movement's (UNM) candidate. The UNM and one other major anti-government party believed that the parliamentary election results had been rigged. And so, on November 22, as President Shevardnadze was addressing Parliament, Saakashvili and some supporters burst into the chamber carrying red roses.

Bodyguards hustled the president away, but within hours of meeting with Saakashvili and another opposition leader, Shevardnadze announced his resignation. That night in Tbilisi, Georgia's capital, more than 100,000 citizens enjoyed fireworks and rock music as they celebrated the Rose Revolution.

Another upheaval in the Caucasus, the Pink (or Tulip) Revolution, succeeded in deposing President Askar Akayev of Kyrgyzstan and his government in the spring of 2005. The proximate cause,

ABOVE: **Hundreds sing songs in Ukraine for the first anniversary of the Orange Revolution, 2005.**

ABOVE: **Mir-Hossein Mousavi supporters rally in Tehran (Green Revolution), 2009.**

a controversial parliamentary election, had been preceded by unrest going back to 2002, during Akayev's third and final term as president.

As president, Akayev had favored privatization of land and other assets, an unusual stance among Central Asian leaders. He also favored his own family, to the extent of facilitating control of forty-two business enterprises by his relatives, and by March 2005, thousands of opponents of the regime were protesting corruption, as well as fraud in the preceding month's

elections and instances of state-authorized violence. On March 20, with protesters in control of all the large cities in southern Kyrgyzstan, opposition leaders demanded that Akayev step down. On March 22, he refused, his derision reflected in the name he gave the movement against him: the Tulip Revolution.

Obligated to deal with his opponents' assertions of election fraud, Akayev called for an investigation, dismissed high-level officials, and sent out riot police to calm ongoing protests.

On March 24, he and his family departed for Russia via Kazakhstan. Then the prime minister resigned and opposition cadres took over such state services as television broadcasting.

Soon after, the Kyrgyzstan Supreme Court invalidated the election results, clearing the way for Kurmanbek Bakiyev of the People's Movement of Kyrgyzstan to become acting prime minister and acting president. Mob violence, which had developed in late March, was quelled, and on April 11, Akayev's recently

The Fight for Peace and Freedom

signed resignation statement was ratified by the country's interim parliament, completing the revolution.

The Orange Revolution in Ukraine (November 2004–January 2005) took place in an atmosphere of government corruption and criminality during the administration of outgoing president Leonid Kuchma. In the presidential election of 2004, the sitting prime minister, Viktor Yanukovych, was the announced winner, but leaders of the Orange Revolution, supported by international election monitors, had the results annulled on the grounds of fraud. The winner of the revote was the Orange candidate Viktor Yushchenko, who enjoyed nationalist support as well as a reputation for integrity.

Yanukovych ran again in 2010 and soundly defeated Yushchenko, whom many voters believed leaned too far to the right. However, Yushchenko declared a victory for a key Orange value, free and fair elections. Russia's move into the Crimean region of Ukraine in February 2014 put Orange partisans even more out of favor.

A color revolution that has often been called a civil rights revolution shook Iran for nearly eight months in the wake of that country's 2009 presidential election. As in Georgia, Kyrgyzstan, and Ukraine, election fraud was the precipitating cause, but the protest also reflected popular resentment over other aspects of the regime.

An announcement early in the night of June 12 that incumbent president Mahmoud Ahmadinejad's tally exceeded 60 percent of the votes met disbelief from supporters of his opponents, Mir-Hossein Mousavi, the Green candidate, and Shia cleric Mehdi Karroubi, of the National Trust Party. The unpopular president's economic policies had led to inflation that hurt all Iranians, and some conservative and moderate Muslim leaders believed he threatened their power.

Protests all over the country began in earnest the next day, when Ahmadinejad's win was confirmed, and on June 15, millions rallied in Tehran. Regime response to the mainly peaceful demonstrations was heavy-handed from the first, as police and the Basij, Iran's paramilitary force, beat protesters mercilessly. At least 4,000 were arrested, jailed, and sometimes tortured. There were shootings as well.

On June 20, Neda Agha-Soltan bled out in the street; the young woman's death, captured on videotape, has been witnessed by untold millions. And for more than six months, the revolution waxed and waned. The end of the protest was officially set as February 11, 2010, the thirty-first anniversary of the overthrow of the shah and the day on which Ahmadinejad announced that Iran had become a nuclear power. ∎

EGYPTIAN
REVOLUTION OF 2011

" "

We are not going to leave the square. We want the army on our side, but the army must realize the people's revolution is here to stay.

—METWALY FARGHALI

TOP: **Anti-government protesters in Tahrir Square in Cairo, Egypt.** BOTTOM: **Protesters wave national flags and chant.**

THE IMPETUS FOR the movement that resulted in the resignation of Egyptian president Hosni Mubarak after nearly a month of nationwide protests began before many of the first demonstrators in Cairo's Tahrir Square were born. For millions of others, thirty years of increasingly repressive rule under Mubarak had sufficed to make activists out of people representing a cross section of Egyptian society: from wealthy Google executive Wael Ghonim and International Atomic Energy Agency (IAEA) director Mohamed ElBaradei to members of lawyers' associations, shopkeepers (the *bazaari*), university students, the urban poor, and the even poorer Bedouin.

Conditions were grim: poverty exacerbated by high food prices and high unemployment; government corruption that tolerated injustice everywhere; and high inflation that touched all but the very wealthy. Activists called for Egyptians to observe a Day of Rage, issued on January 20, 2011, and it was met with enthusiastic response. On January 25, a national holiday to honor police forces, thousands marched in Cairo, in the Nile Delta, and in the south. The protesters chanted "Down with Mubarak!" and 50,000 occupied Cairo's Tahrir Square.

> "There are no heroes; we are all heroes on the street."
>
> —WAEL GHONIM

The first wave of activists had the advantage of a hastily published pamphlet titled *How to Protest Intelligently*. This field manual contained both practical and tactical information, including advice on preparing for encounters with riot police. The information was useful for protesters, as the tear gas and water cannons that greeted the first day's protesters were later supplemented by beatings and gunfire.

ElBaradei arrived in Cairo on January 27 to participate in the protests and to announce that he would lead the transition government the protesters were demanding as a follow-up to their first demand that Mubarak resign. Also on that day, the government disrupted Facebook and Twitter, a tacit acknowledgment of the services' usefulness to the protesters.

The protests continued and spread, and on January 29, Mubarak, from an unknown location, dismissed his cabinet and declined to step down. He repeated his refusal to resign two days later, attempting to sweeten the message by pledging not to seek a seventh term as president in the September election. The protesters found the offer unacceptable; ElBaradei publicly called it deceptive. By February 1, estimates of the crowd in Tahrir Square topped one million.

Government attempts at conciliation continued as well. Between February 6 and 9, an Al Jazeera correspondent was released after a brief detention, and Google's Wael Ghonim was released after more than a week in a secret location; thirty-four others, including members of the Muslim Brotherhood, also received their freedom.

On February 10, Mubarak's final speech reiterated his vow not to run for reelection, plus a promise to assist in a peaceful transition at the proper time. The public rejected this offer in no uncertain terms. Photographs of the crowd in Tahrir Square show rows of people waving footgear in the air—the traditional Arab insult of hitting a despised person with the sole of one's shoe, which is presumed to be covered with excrement.

Tens of thousands all over Egypt protested on the next day, and Mubarak resigned, giving power to the army. February 12 was devoted to celebration, but on February 13 protesters returned to the Square to begin cleaning up. The next day, the protest was over. It was time for a transition.

A democratic election held during the spring of 2012 gave Egypt a new president, Mohamed Morsi, a former member of parliament who had been arrested along with other Muslim Brotherhood leaders at the height of the revolution of 2011. His administration was soon marred by protests and the return of tents to Tahrir Square. Critics, including ElBaradei, believed

RIGHT: **Egyptian protesters join in prayer at Tahrir Square.**

the president had personally taken too many powers. Secular Egyptians worried about his pronounced Islamist stance.

On June 30, 2013, exactly a year after Morsi's inauguration, as many as 14 million protesters nationwide called for his resignation. The coup, led by Egyptian Armed Forces general Abdel Fattah al-Sisi, came three days later. Morsi was removed from office, and another transition began.

An appointed interim government, under Adly Mansour, treated Morsi, the Muslim Brotherhood, and its Islamist supporters harshly; a police massacre in August drew international criticism. Thousands who were protesting Morsi's deposition were gunned down in their encampments in Rabaa and Al Nahda Squares. Afterward, anti-Brotherhood Egyptians asked al-Sisi to resign from the army and run for president. He complied, winning the election with 93 percent of the vote. ■

HOW TO GET INVOLVED

IN THE FIGHT FOR PEACE AND FREEDOM

RESEARCH · SPEAK OUT · VOLUNTEER
TALK · LISTEN · DONATE · MARCH · VOTE
CALL YOUR LOCAL REPRESENTATIVES
START YOUR OWN ORGANIZATION!

INDIVIDUALLY AND COLLECTIVELY, at home and abroad, Americans have fought for peace and justice since colonial times. While the accessibility of justice has been improved domestically, in much of the world peace is uncertain or absent altogether. Getting involved often means becoming active in one of the many organizations devoted to peace or refugee relief. Some activists prefer to monitor the international situation and donate to programs that target urgent needs of particular concern to themselves. There is no single best way to get involved.

Not all efforts to achieve peace in a country or a region take the form of protest marches or aid missions to war zones. The Friends Committee on National Legislation, whose motto is "A Quaker Lobby in the Public Interest," has a broad mandate:

We seek a world free of war and the threat of war.
We seek a society with equity and justice for all.
We seek a community where every person's potential
   may be fulfilled.
We seek an earth restored.

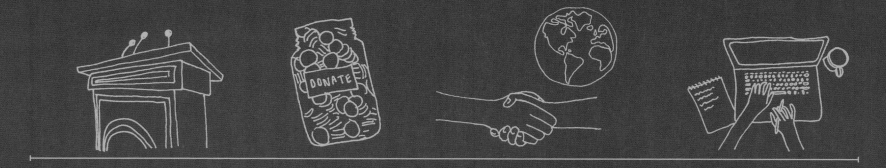

The group's aims are listed on its website (fcnl.org), along with ways for volunteers to help.

Among the organizations working at the grassroots level is Peace Action, which has opposed the spread and use of nuclear weapons since 1957 (when it was called SANE). The group speaks out against U.S. military actions abroad and believes that the goals of slowing climate change and securing peace are inseparable. Peace Action's New York and Massachusetts chapters are very active; the website (Peace-Action.org) describes opportunities to volunteer and otherwise get involved.

The members of Veterans for Peace, founded in 1985, work to modify policies that risk or sustain wars, focusing on the United States, Israel, and NATO. VFP's opposition to military actions and threats to adversaries sometimes take extreme forms, such as a call to disband NATO. A much-praised project addressed Agent Orange and other toxic herbicides deployed over Southeast Asia during the Vietnam War. Cleanup work in the countries continues, as does assistance to Vietnamese citizens and former U.S. service personnel whose health was affected by the chemicals; in the United States, VFP is lobbying Congress to address those issues. You don't have to be a veteran to help out with VFP programs, which are described on the website (veteransforpeace.org).

For those who want to go beyond marching and lobbying, necessary though these activities are, the International Campaign to Ban Land Mines offers opportunities to clear mines in thirty-five countries abroad and to assist mutilated victims. The website (icbl. org) supplies information about self-education and other qualifications for volunteers.

As with protest efforts in other areas, involvement in the peace movement can come in many forms. A local house of worship may have a small but focused program for helping refugees en route to freedom from war-torn countries. Colleges and universities often sponsor activities in response to a crisis under study by activist faculty. The absence of any such opportunity in your area is a clear challenge to start your own. ∎

THE FIGHT FOR WOMEN'S RIGHTS

1848
The Seneca Falls Convention convenes, and Elizabeth Cady Stanton reads the Declaration of Sentiments.

1903
Women's Trade Union League is founded to support working women.

1920
The Nineteenth Amendment to the U.S. Constitution is ratified, granting all American women the right to vote.

1921
Margaret Sanger founds the American Birth Control League.

1776
Abigail Adams tells John Adams to "remember the ladies" when drafting the Constitution of the United States.

remember the ladies

1838
Widows with children of schooling age in Kentucky are given the right to vote in school board elections.

1869
Wyoming becomes the first state to grant women the right to vote.

1913
The Woman Suffrage Procession parade is held in Washington, DC.

1925
Nellie Tayloe Ross of Wyoming is inaugurated as the first female governor in the United States.

1963

The Equal Pay Act of 1963 is signed into law.

1978

The Pregnancy Discrimination Act of 1978 is passed.

1993

The Supreme Court rules that sexual harassment in the workplace is illegal.

1997

Madeleine Albright is sworn in as the first female secretary of state.

2017

500,000 women march on Washington to protest the Trump administration, joined by millions around the world.

#METOO

1956

Approximately 20,000 women led by the Federation of South African Women and the Women's League of the African National Congress march on Pretoria.

1964

Title VII of the Civil Rights Act of 1964 is signed into law.

1973

The United States Supreme Court issues decision in *Roe v. Wade*.

1984

Geraldine Ferraro is the first female vice presidential candidate on a major party ticket.

1994

The first National Women's Day is celebrated in South Africa under President Nelson Mandela.

2016

Hillary Rodham Clinton becomes the first female presidential candidate for a major political party.

I'm With Her

2017

Congress has a record number of women, with eighty-four female House members and twenty-one female Senators, including the chamber's first Latina, Senator Catherine Cortez Masto.

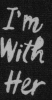

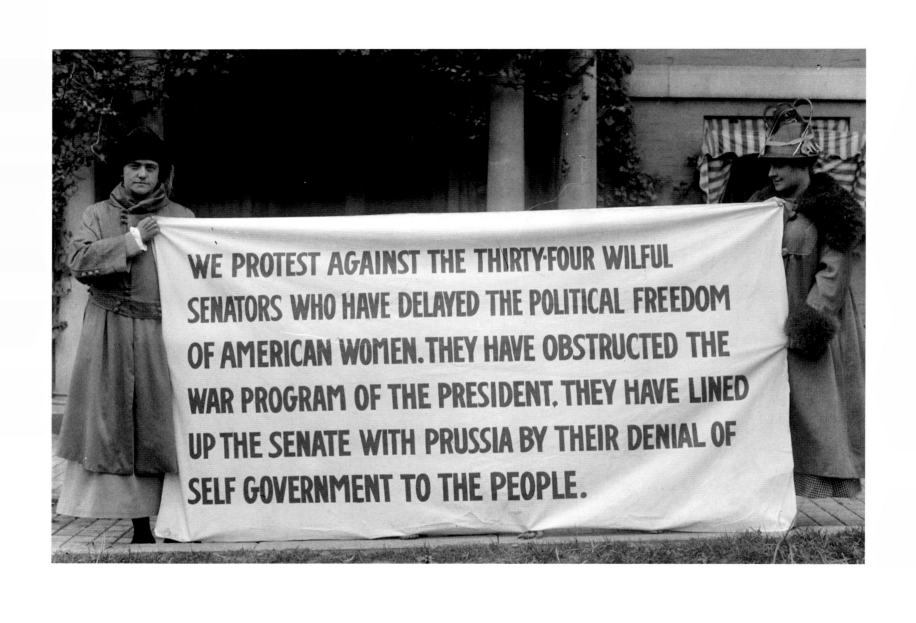

TOP: **Lucretia Mott, 1793-1880.**
BOTTOM: **Elizabeth Cady Stanton, 1815-1902.**
LEFT: **Two suffragists with a sign, 1918.**

WOMEN'S SUFFRAGE

" "

Men, their rights, and nothing more; women,
their rights, and nothing less.

—SUSAN B. ANTHONY

1848, SENECA FALLS

THE SENECA FALLS Convention of 1848, organized by abolitionists Lucretia Mott and Elizabeth Cady Stanton to "discuss the social, civil, and religious condition and rights of women," attracted 200 women as well as a few dozen men. The foundational document, the Declaration of Sentiments and Grievances, used language modeled after the Declaration of Independence to list the injustices U.S. women experienced and to exhort them to organize and petition for their rights. The document, written by Stanton, was discussed in a closed (women only) session on the first day of the convention. It was adopted and signed by men and women alike on the second day.

The second day also saw the passage of resolutions calling for equal rights for women in twelve areas; eleven passed unanimously. However, the ninth resolution stated that the women of the country were duty-bound "to secure to themselves their sacred right to the elective franchise." Many today are surprised to learn that an opponent of the ninth resolution was one of the organizers of the event, Lucretia Mott. Mott, an ardent abolitionist, believed that including women's suffrage in the convention's resolutions would generate opposition that would detract from the other rights everyone agreed on. In a heated debate, one man supported the idea that women should be allowed to vote. He was the abolitionist Frederick Douglass, who had purchased his freedom from slavery only the year before.

Both sides of the debate over the suffrage resolution had valid points. In the United States today, no one would suggest revoking women's right to vote. But Mott was right in the short term in that the public ridicule heaped on the convention as a result of the ninth resolution did lead some early supporters of women's rights to abandon the cause. Nevertheless, for nearly a century, historians have cited that resolution as the beginning of the women's suffrage movement. ■

"THE RIGHT WAY IS NOT ALWAYS THE POPULAR AND EASY WAY. STANDING FOR RIGHT WHEN IT IS UNPOPULAR IS A TRUE TEST OF MORAL CHARACTER."
–MARGARET CHASE SMITH

TOP: **Inez Milholland Boissevain riding a white horse through the Women's Suffrage Parade.** RIGHT: **Suffragist with her homemade banner in the parade.**

WOMEN'S SUFFRAGE PARADE IN WASHINGTON, DC, 1913

LAWYER INEZ MILHOLLAND Boissevain was one of four mounted heralds of the Suffrage Parade, held in Washington, DC, on March 3, 1913. The heralds preceded more than 5,000 marchers along Pennsylvania Avenue, drawing nationwide attention to the movement to achieve votes for women. To fund the occasion, the National Woman Suffrage Association (NWSA), led by Elizabeth Cady Stanton and Susan B. Anthony, raised more than $14,000 (equivalent to over $300,000 today). The Suffrage Parade was a signal event in the formal struggle, by then sixty-five years old, to gain for women that fundamental right. ∎

> "I would have girls regard themselves not as adjectives but as nouns."
>
> —ELIZABETH CADY STANTON

WINNING THE VOTE AT LAST

WOMEN COULD VOTE in Wyoming, Colorado, Utah, and Idaho by 1896. But many throughout the country were opposed, and in 1913 hundreds of women were injured at the NWSA parade. After eighteen months of picketing in front of the White House and a hunger strike, Alice Paul and other suffrage leaders were jailed and force-fed. Despite these setbacks, suffragists persisted, and, in 1919, the Senate passed the Nineteenth Amendment, granting women the right to vote. Ratified in 1920 by two-thirds of the states, women's suffrage became the law of the land. ∎

WOMAN'S JOURNAL
AND SUFFRAGE NEWS

VOL. XLIV. NO. 10   SATURDAY, MARCH 8, 1913   FIVE CENTS

PARADE STRUGGLES TO VICTORY DESPITE DISGRACEFUL SCENES

Nation Aroused by Open Insults to Women—Cause Wins Popular Sympathy—Congress Orders Investigation—Striking Object Lesson

Washington has been disgraced. Equal suffrage has scored a great victory. Thousands of indifferent women have been aroused. Influential men are incensed and the United States Senate demands an investigation of the treatment given the suffragists at the National Capital on Monday.

Ten thousand women from all over the country had planned a magnificent parade and pageant to take place in Washington on March 3. Artists, pageant leaders, designers, women of influence and renown were ready to give a wonderful and beautiful piece of suffrage work to the public that would throng the National Capital for the inauguration festivities. The suffragists were ready; the whole procession started down Pennsylvania avenue, when the police protection, that had been promised, failed them, and a disgraceful scene followed. The crowd surged into the space which had been marked off for the paraders, and the leaders of the suffrage movement were compelled to push their way through a mob of the worst element in Washington and vicinity. Women were spit upon, slapped in the face, tripped up, pelted with burning cigar stubs, and insulted by jeers and obscene language too vile to print or repeat.

The cause of all the trouble is apparent when the facts are known. The police authorities in Washington opposed every attempt to have a suffrage parade at all. Having been forbidden a place in the inaugural procession, the suffragists asked to have a procession of their own on March 3. They were finally told that they could have a procession but that it could not be on Pennsylvania avenue, but must be on a side street. At last they got permission to have the suffrage parade on the avenue, and asked that traffic be excluded from the street during the parade. For a long time this was denied, and only on Saturday were they successful.

Everything was at last arranged; it was a glorious day; ten thousand women were ready to do their part to make the parade beautiful to behold, to make it a credit to womanhood and to demonstrate the strength of the movement for their enfranchisement. The police were determined, however, and they had their way. Their attempt to afford the marchers protection and keep the space of the avenue free for the suffrage procession was the flimsiest sham. Police officers stood by with folded arms and grinned while the picked women of the land were insulted and roughly abused by an ignorant and uncouth mob.

Miss Alice Paul and other suffragists were compelled to drive their automobiles down the avenue to separate the crowds so the suffragists—with the banners and floats could pass. The police officials say their force was inadequate to handle the crowds, but it is noted that there was no disorder on the avenue during the inaugural procession. It is stated that federal troops were offered to the chief of police for the suffrage procession, but that he refused their aid. At any rate, assistance was finally called from Fort Myer and mounted soldiers drove back the crowd so that a straggling line of marchers could pass through.

Not only were the suffragists bitterly disappointed in having the effect

(Continued on Page 78)

AMENDMENT WINS IN NEW JERSEY

Easy Victory in Assembly 45 to 5—Equal Suffrage Enthusiasm Runs High

The New Jersey Legislature passed the woman suffrage amendment in the Assembly last week by a vote of 46 to 5. The Senate had already voted favorably 14 to 5.

A large delegation of suffragists crowded the galleries, and when the overwhelming vote was announced there was a scene of great enthusiasm. Women stood in their seats and waved handkerchiefs and "votes for women" flags and cheered themselves hoarse.

Dr. Jekyll Becomes Mr. Hyde Opposition was confined exclusively to the old sentimental arguments.

(Continued on Page 79)

MICHIGAN AGAIN CAMPAIGN STATE

Senate Passes Suffrage Amendment 26 to 5 and Battle Is Now On

Michigan is again a campaign State after a short lapse of four months. The amendment will go to the voters on April 7. The State-wide feeling that the women were defrauded of victory last fall will help the suffragists.

The final action of the Legislature was taken last week, when the Senate, by a vote of 26 to 5, passed the suffrage amendment, with a slight amendment to make the requirements for foreign-born women the same as those for male immigrants.

Governor Watches Debate

The debate in the Senate lasted an hour and a quarter, and was characterized by the persistent efforts of Senator Weadock and a few others to lack on crippling amendments. Several suggestions, including the disabling of women for holding office or serving on juries, were voted down in quick succession.

Gov. Ferris was among the visitors who crowded the chamber and gallery. Mrs. Clara B. Arthur, Mrs. Thomas E. Henderson and Mrs. Wilbur Brotherton, of Detroit; Mrs. Jennie Law Hardy, of Tecumseh, and other State leaders were present, supported by a large delegation of Lansing suffragists.

The final stand of the opposition was made by Senator Martha in the hope of putting off the submission till November, 1914, but this also failed. Of the five who opposed the measure on the final roll-call, three were from Detroit.

A complete campaign of organization and education has been mapped out by the State Association. The

(Continued on Page 74.)

General Rosalie Jones in Pilgrim Costume; Miss Inez Milholland on White Steed Leading the Parade; One of the Scores of Imposing Floats; One View of the Procession

TOP: **FSAW members give thumbs up after delivering a petition to the Union Buildings in Pretoria, South Africa, 1955.**
BOTTOM: **Winnie Madikizela-Mandela, the ANC president, leads a march through Pretoria to celebrate National Woman's Day, 1996.**
LEFT: **Front page of the *Woman's Journal and Suffrage News* reporting the events of the suffrage parade, 1913.**

SOUTH AFRICAN
WOMEN'S MARCH

" "

Freedom cannot be achieved unless the women have been emancipated from all forms of oppression.

—NELSON MANDELA

DURING SOUTH AFRICAN Apartheid in the 1950s, the white authorities wanted to ban African women from living in the towns unless they had permission to work there. To achieve that result, they required women "unqualified" to live in the towns to carry a pass to travel. Passes had to be renewed every month by purchasing a replacement, compounding the difficulty women faced in arranging family visits to husbands with jobs in town. There were sporadic protests, some leading to the arrest of female leaders. In 1955, however, the Federation of South African Women (FSAW) and the Women's League of the African National Congress (ANC) organized a definitive protest march in Pretoria. Along with committing to publicize the event among women in both towns and townships, the FSAW responded to the male authorities' belief that a woman's place is in the kitchen by proclaiming that a woman's place is "everywhere."

The march took place on August 9, 1956. Most of the participants were "coloured," the term then used to refer to native peoples as well as emigrants from Asian and South Asian countries. White women also swelled the ranks of the marchers, who numbered 20,000. The women proceeded to the prime minister's office, only to be told that he wasn't available to accept their petition against carrying of passes; the petition had 100,000 signatures. The women stood in silence for half an hour, until at last the prime minister's secretary came out to take custody of the document.

The impressively peaceful, well-organized act of defiance by women generated respect among the men of the African National Congress and other anti-Apartheid groups. This, in turn, opened the way for a marginalized group to participate more fully in the battle for freedom, democracy, and an end to Apartheid. Nelson Mandela became president of the country in 1994, and in 1995 the first National Women's Day was celebrated on August 9. ∎

The Power of Protest

SECOND-WAVE FEMINISM

" "

We are volcanoes. When we women offer our experience as our truth, as human truth, all the maps change. There are new mountains.

—URSULA K. LE GUIN

TOP: **Female employees of Ford Motors attend a conference on equal rights in the auto industry, 1968.**
BOTTOM: **N.O.W. members picket outside the White House for the passage of the Equal Rights Amendment, 1969.**
LEFT: **Crowds gather at the Women's March on Pretoria, 1955.**

THE DECADES BETWEEN 1960 and 1980 are often referred to as the "second wave" of feminism, following the battles for suffrage and property rights, which constituted the first wave. "Women's liberation" was the umbrella term for the movement urging women to seek empowerment at home and with respect to their bodies, as well as equality in schools and colleges, in the workplace, in politics and civic life, and in the arts and literature. Feminists identified the role of sexist language in perpetuating the tradition of female subservience and made progress in eliminating it, at least among women. The term "rape culture" was introduced in the United States, and the concept was defined in books, on film, and in journal papers.

The often-cited abortion case, *Roe v. Wade* [see page 55], which many view as emblematic of "women's liberation," is only one facet of the overall goal of reproductive freedom; other goals include economic self-determination, bodily autonomy, and equality in medical care. In fact, the 1973 Supreme Court decision does not declare a right to abortion on demand, and subsequent rulings have narrowed the access to this procedure.

Other important gains during the second wave include the Equal Pay Act of 1963. This amendment to an existing statute (the Fair Labor Standards Act) prohibited employers from paying unequal wages on the basis of gender as long as employees were doing substantially the same work and employed in the same establishment. The law was a good first step, beneficial to many women; others, however, learned that the protection was not complete.

Further legislation on women's pay was written into the Civil Rights Act of 1964, Title VII of which makes it illegal for employers to decide not to hire any person, or to discharge him or her, on grounds of "race, color, religion, sex, or national origin." The act also covers terms of employment and workplace conditions. The Age Discrimination in Employment Act of 1967 extends its protections to women as well.

The Pregnancy Discrimination Act of 1978 was another welcome extension of Title VII. This law expands the existing language "because of sex" or "on the basis of sex" to include acts of sex discrimination "on the basis of pregnancy, childbirth, or related medical conditions." Women to whom those conditions apply may not be deprived of fringe benefits available to other employees not being discriminated against.

Women's studies gained a foothold in academia in 1969, when Cornell University offered the country's first accredited course in the subject. A year later, San Diego State College (now University) established an entire women's studies program. Doctoral programs, from Emory University to Kabul University, did not appear for decades, but the path had been established.

The chant is familiar to anyone who watches television in an English-speaking country: for years, feminist protesters have repeated again and

again, "Our bodies, our rights!" However, it would be a mistake to assume that the statement applies only to abortion and access to the contraceptive device or drug of a woman's choice.

The human rights organization Amnesty International, which recognizes that every person, regardless of gender, has rights with respect to his or her body, has insisted that these wide-ranging rights are deserving of respect and protection.

Amnesty offers a reminder that one's bodily rights are subject to controls from multiple authorities and that the right to choose is often circumscribed by laws, mooting, for many women, the whole concept of choice. Amnesty's list of rights associated with one's body is comprehensive; the rights themselves remain beyond the reach of some or most women all over the world. ■

LEFT: **A woman cheers at an equal pay demonstration in Trafalgar Square, London, 1969.**
RIGHT: **Lillian Garland, who took maternity leave and lost her job, standing with her lawyer and feminist activist Betty Friedan on the steps of the Supreme Court, 1986.**

TOP: **Justice Harry A. Blackmun, 1976.**
BOTTOM: **Pro-choice and pro-life activists clash outside of the Supreme Court after the *Roe* ruling, 1973.**
LEFT: **Attorney Gloria Allred and Norma McCorvey, a.k.a. Jane Roe, 1989.**

ROE V. WADE

" "

No woman can call herself free who does not own and control her body.

—MARGARET SANGER

AS RECENTLY AS the early 1970s, opinions on the issue of abortion were seen mainly in terms of the positions identified as "pro-life," or against abortion, and "pro-choice," or favoring a woman's right to decide whether to continue a pregnancy. Matters came to a head in 1973 with the Supreme Court's controversial decision in the case of *Roe v. Wade*.

The Court declared abortion a fundamental right. Narrowly speaking, the justices pronounced unconstitutional most of a Texas law that had prevented the plaintiff from getting an abortion in 1970. The Court was divided 7–2; the author of the opinion, Justice Harry Blackmun, had been assigned to that case because he had once served as counsel to the Mayo Clinic. However, his ruling was based less on medical grounds than on the idea that the First, Fourth, Ninth, and Fourteenth Amendments to the Constitution guarantee a woman's right to privacy in accordance with existing earlier Court decisions.

Blackmun elaborated by stating

that U.S. law supports a "zone of privacy...broad enough to encompass a woman's decision whether or not to terminate her pregnancy." At the time, many Americans believed that decisions on, for example, marriage and contraception, were private activities. However, many others did not support interracial marriage or free access to contraceptives, although state laws banning both practices had been declared unconstitutional. The Texas law, which did allow abortion to save the life of the mother, again mirrored the belief of almost everyone in the country, except those who held abortion under any circumstances to be morally unacceptable.

One Supreme Court dissenter, Byron White, viewed the *Roe* decision as judicial overreach, an override of a state law without constitutional backing. In addition, his ruling suggests that, like many Americans, he felt concern for the rights of the fetus as well as those of the mother. The other dissenter, William Rehnquist, had procedural and technical grounds for his opinion that had little

resonance with pro-choice women and men, nor did they interest proponents of the pro-life position who objected to abortion on moral grounds.

Most of the vigorous pro-life supporters were members of Christian denominations or affiliated with the informal political coalition known as the Christian Right, which reacted to *Roe* by taking a strong stand against abortion in many or all cases. At the time, the Roman Catholic Church, as well as organizations run by lay Catholics, opposed all forms of abortion, without exception. The Christian Right held to the view that life begins at conception, and therefore abortion is murder.

Pro-choice advocates, buoyed by the Supreme Court's ruling, had been supported all along by Planned Parenthood, the organization now known as NARAL (formerly the National Association for the Repeal of Abortion Laws), the National Organization for Women (NOW), and the ACLU.

"Jane Roe," the famous plaintiff in *Roe v. Wade*, was an impoverished young Texan woman named Norma

McCorvey who had been barred by state law from securing an abortion in 1970. By the time the U.S. Supreme Court had ruled on the case in 1973, McCorvey had delivered the child and completed adoption proceedings. She never appeared in court or at a hearing and was not asked to testify, nor was she involved in the Supreme Court case in any way.

Texas law in 1970 criminalized all abortions not "procured or attempted by medical advice for the purpose of saving the life of the mother." A three-judge state court ruled that language of the law was overly broad, an opinion that was confirmed in the 1973 opinion written by Justice Harry Blackmun. His introduction to the ruling notes the controversial nature of the subject:

"We forthwith acknowledge our awareness of the sensitive and emotional nature of the abortion controversy, of the vigorous opposing views, even among physicians, and of the deep and seemingly absolute convictions that the subject inspires.... In addition, population growth, pollution, poverty, and [other issues] tend to complicate and not to simplify the problem."

Although the Court's decision—that the Texas law was unconstitutional—was ultimately based on "constitutional measurement, free of emotion and of predilection," the justices had studied social and medical materials in reaching their opinion. Rejecting an earlier contention that the Ninth Amendment, reserving to "the people" rights not enumerated in the first seven Amendments, Blackmun declared that McCorvey's right to privacy, deemed to be implicit in the Fourteenth Amendment guaranteeing due process of the law, had been violated by the Texas law.

Liberal law professors, including Laurence Tribe, Alan Dershowitz, and Cass Sunstein, criticized the decision as too vague. Ruth Bader Ginsburg, not yet a member of the Court, objected for other reasons, pointing out that the ruling had the effect of usurping a popular movement to liberalize abortion law through legislation.

"FOR WHAT IS THIS BAN ON ABORTION? IT IS A SEXUAL TABOO, IT IS THE TERROR THAT WOMEN SHOULD EXPERIMENT AND ENJOY FREELY, WITHOUT PUNISHMENT. IT IS A SURVIVAL OF THE VEILED FACE, OF THE BARRED WINDOW AND THE LOCKED DOOR, OF BURNING, BRANDING, MUTILATION, AND STONING; OF ALL THE PAIN AND FEAR INFLICTED EVER SINCE THE GRIP OF OWNERSHIP AND SUPERSTITION CAME DOWN ON WOMEN, THOUSANDS OF YEARS AGO."

–STELLA BROWNE

ABOVE: **Protesters wave signs at a Right to Life demonstration at the White House, 1978.**
LEFT: **Norma McCorvey and Gloria Allred are greeted by a crowd as they gather at a pro-choice rally.**

Moreover, Ginsburg read the decision as being centered not on women but on physicians and their freedom to practice their profession.

Only sixteen years later, the Supreme Court moved to narrow the parameters of *Roe* in *Webster v. Reproductive Health Service,* a case involving Missouri state law. This decision did impose restrictions on a doctor's approach to treating patients who sought abortions, and it limited the venues for performing the procedure in a way likely to prevent poor women from ending their pregnancies. Additional restrictions and requirements of women were imposed by *Planned Parenthood v. Casey* (1992). *Stenberg v. Carhart* (2000) stamped as unconstitutional a Nebraska law banning pro-life-branded "partial-birth" abortions. In 2007, however, *Gonzales v. Carhart* upheld an act of Congress, the Partial-Birth Abortion Ban of 2003; it was another disappointment for many feminists.

The final decade of second-wave feminism in North America was paralleled by the commencement of that period in Turkey and in Israel. Important advances were achieved in France and Japan with respect to equal pay for women who worked at companies employing at least fifty people, and in Japan, which banned several forms of gender discrimination in the workplace. ■

LEFT: **Margaret Sanger has her mouth covered in protest of not being allowed to talk about birth control in Boston, 1929.**

"REPRODUCTIVE FREEDOM IS NOT JUST THE ABILITY NOT TO HAVE A CHILD THROUGH BIRTH CONTROL. IT'S THE ABILITY TO HAVE ONE IF AND WHEN YOU WANT ONE."

–PAMELA MADSEN

IT'S YOUR BODY.
KNOW YOUR RIGHTS!

WE ALL HAVE the right to make decisions about our own health, body, sexuality, and reproductive life without fear, coercion, violence, or discrimination. But all over the world, people's freedom to make these decisions is controlled by the state, medical professionals, and even their own families. Criminal law and punitive sanctions are frequently used to control such choices. In the end, many people are prevented from making any choice at all.

SEXUAL AND REPRODUCTIVE RIGHTS MEAN YOU HAVE THE RIGHT TO:

Have access to fact-based, comprehensive sex education.

Access sexual and reproductive health services, including contraception.

Decide if you want to have children, when you want to have them, and how many.

Choose your intimate partner and whether you want to marry and when.

Make decisions about your own health, body, sexual life, and identity without fear, coercion, criminalization, or discrimination.

Live free from violence, including rape and other sexual violence (e.g., female genital mutilation/cutting, forced pregnancy, forced abortion, forced sterilization, and forced marriage).

Access safe abortion services at a minimum in cases of rape or incest, when the life or health of the pregnant person is at risk, or when there is severe or fatal fetal impairment.

Live free from discrimination based on your sex, gender, sexuality, or perceived identity.

TOP: **Lawyer Brenda Feigen Fasteau raising her hand in argument during a National Women's Political Caucus meeting, 1972.**
BOTTOM: **Jimmy Carter signing legislation that gives a time extension for the ratification of the Equal Rights Amendment, 1978.**
LEFT: **National Organization for Women leaders Dr. Kathryn F. Clarenbach and Betty Friedan at a meeting, 1968.**

WORKING WOMEN OF THE '80s

" "

People ask me sometimes, "When will there be enough women on the Court?" And my answer is: "When there are nine."

—RUTH BADER GINSBURG

RADCLIFFE COLLEGE HAD begun to merge with Harvard in 1963, a transitional process that was completed in 1977, and Vassar had become coeducational in 1969, but the other prestigious northeastern all-female universities once known as the Seven Sisters did not follow suit. Elsewhere in the country, the Mississippi University for Women became coeducational after a 1982 Supreme Court ruling that the school's admissions policy violated the Fourteenth Amendment rights of men.

The eighties are seen, in retrospect, as having largely ignored poor and working-class women, as well as LGBT women. In 1982, the Equal Rights Amendment, drafted by Alice Paul and Crystal Eastman and presented in 1923, failed to become part of the Constitution because five states had rescinded their votes. Proponents of the amendment were unable to meet Congress's extended deadline for making up the number.

Feminist writings included writers of nonfiction and fiction by authors as diverse as Indira Gandhi ("True

> **"I believe that the rights of women and girls is the unfinished business of the twenty-first century."**
>
> —HILLARY CLINTON

Liberation of Women"), bell hooks (*Ain't I a Woman? Black Women and Feminism*), Alice Walker (*The Color Purple*), Gloria Steinem (*Outrageous Acts and Everyday Rebellions* and "If Men Could Menstruate"), Adrienne Rich (*Blood, Bread, and Poetry: Selected Prose*), Catharine McKinnon (*Feminism Unmodified: Discourses on Life and Law*), and Ursula K. Le Guin (*Dancing at the Edge of the World*).

However, the 1986 Supreme Court case *Meritor Savings Bank v. Vinson* supplied legal backing for women who, like plaintiff Mechelle Vinson, were subjected to sexual harassment at work. In a ruling that gave legal credence to the term "hostile work environment," the protections of Title VII of the Civil Rights Act of 1964 were expanded to cover "the entire spectrum of disparate treatment of men and women in employment." The ruling, written by Justice William Rehnquist, noted that the Equal Employment Opportunity Commission had cited sexual harassment that was "severe or pervasive" and led to noneconomic injury as a form of sex discrimination.

Vinson's horrifying experience at Meritor surely meets the Court's criteria of unwelcome behaviors based on her gender and creation of a work environment that was abusive as well as hostile. The plaintiff testified that Sidney Taylor, the bank's vice president, had raped her several times, in addition to demanding sexual favors from her at work that included dozens of acts of sexual intercourse. Her painful ordeal and subsequent legal action has resulted in better on-the-job treatment for countless women and a route to vindication for many others.

Toward the end of the twentieth century, the Federal Glass Ceiling Commission of the United States released a sixty-five-page report of its recommendations for breaking that very ceiling, which it described as "the unseen, yet unbreachable barrier that keeps minorities and women from rising to the upper rungs of the corporate ladder, regardless of their qualifications or achievements." The 1995 document, titled "A Solid Investment: Making Full Use of the Nation's Human Capital," calls on America's corporate leaders to demonstrate awareness that diversity at management and decision-making levels is essential for the country's long-term success in the marketplace, both at home and globally. ∎

EVENTS OF 1986: THE LAUGHS, THE TEARS, THE TRIUMPHS

Ms.

NEW AWARD
INTERNATIONAL
WOMAN OF THE YEAR
SOUTH AFRICA'S
WINNIE MANDELA

WOMEN
THE YEA

SHARON GLESS
TYNE DALY
JAN KEMP
MARGARET ATWOOD

SISTER DARLENE
NICGORSKI
SARABETH EASON
BARBARA MIKULSKI
DOLLY PARTON

MARY FRANCES BERRY
ANN BANCROFT
VICKI FRANKOVICH
LINDA WACHNER

RAPE CULTURE

"RAPE CULTURE" IS the term that emerged in the 1970s, during the second wave of feminism, to describe an environment, large or small, in which rape is prevalent. One characteristic of such an environment is the normalization of sexual violence against women, accompanied by a tendency to excuse this crime in the media and elsewhere. Symptoms of a rape culture include widespread use of misogynistic language, routine objectification of women's bodies, and glamorized displays of sexual violence; as a result, the rights and safety of women are degraded.

The Women's Center at Marshall University in Huntington, West Virginia, lists some of the symptoms of rape culture:

⇒ Blaming the victim ("She asked for it!")
⇒ Trivializing sexual assault ("Boys will be boys!")
⇒ Sexually explicit jokes
⇒ Tolerance of sexual harassment
⇒ Inflating false rape report statistics
⇒ Publicly scrutinizing a victim's dress, mental state, motives, and history

> "THIS PHRASE [RAPE CULTURE] DENOTES A CULTURE
> WHERE WE ARE INUNDATED, IN DIFFERENT WAYS, BY THE
> IDEA THAT MALE AGGRESSION AND VIOLENCE TOWARD
> WOMEN IS ACCEPTABLE AND OFTEN INEVITABLE."
> —ROXANE GAY

⇨ Gratuitous gendered violence in movies and television

⇨ Defining "manhood" as dominant and sexually aggressive

⇨ Defining "womanhood" as submissive and sexually passive

⇨ Pressure on men to "score"

⇨ Pressure on women to not appear "cold"

⇨ Assuming only promiscuous women get raped

⇨ Assuming that men don't get raped or that only "weak" men get raped

⇨ Refusing to take rape accusations seriously

⇨ Teaching women to avoid getting raped instead of teaching men not to rape

For several reasons, the fallout from rape culture seldom makes the news beyond the locality in which an incident occurs. For one thing, of the fifteen symptoms listed above, sexual harassment is a crime only in the workplace. The trivialization of sexual assault and its corollary, the refusal to take rape accusations seriously, go a long way toward discouraging sexually abused women from filing formal complaints.

When a victim files charges of sexual assault, often only after being urged repeatedly by people advocating for him or her, the result is likely to be disappointing. A particularly discouraging example is the case of Brock Allen Turner, a champion swimmer for Stanford University, who was found guilty on three charges of felony sexual assault of the same woman in 2016. Although by California law he could have spent fourteen years in prison, the prosecutor asked for only six years; the judge's sentence was six months, and Turner was free in three. The case shocked the whole country. Campaigns for the judge to resign or face recall were unsuccessful. However, the California legislature passed two bills modifying state law on sexual assault to increase the mandatory minimum sentence in such cases and to expand the definition of rape. ■

TOP: **Cecile Richards, Planned Parenthood president, 2012.**
BOTTOM: **National cochairs of the Women's March—Tamika Mallory, Linda Sarsour, Bob Bland, and Carmen Perez—pose during New York Fashion Week, 2017.**
LEFT: **Protesters crowd for the Women's March on Washington.**

WOMEN'S MARCH
ON WASHINGTON

" "

We are mothers. We are caregivers. We are artists. We are activists. We are entrepreneurs, doctors, leaders of industry and technology. Our potential is unlimited. We rise.

—ALICIA KEYS

IN 2016, MANY had hoped that cracks in the glass ceiling would be crowned by the election of Hillary Clinton as the first female president of the United States. High enthusiasm for the former first lady could be seen on the memetic level: "I'm with Her" graphics appeared everywhere, and later, repeating Donald Trump's remark addressed to her during a presidential debate, many adult women proudly wore "Nasty Woman" T-shirts. While the triumph of having a female candidate at all should not be dismissed, upon the election of Donald Trump as president, the response by women globally was roaring and immediate.

More than half a million protesters thronged the streets of Washington, DC, on January 21, 2017, one day after the inauguration of Donald J. Trump as president. Sister marches took place all over the country, from Boston, New York, and Chicago to Stamford, CT, and Fargo, ND, to tiny Zebulon, GA (population 1,156), where thirty-five people, including a child, protested in the rain. International protests spanned the globe. In addition to London, Paris, Berlin, and other major European cities, protesters gathered in Mexico City and Antarctica; in South Africa, Kenya, and Malawi; in Kosovo and in Czechia.

Participation worldwide has been estimated at 4.6 million. Throughout the United States, crowds exceeded expectations. Several thousand counterprotesters at the march in Washington were swallowed up by the hundred thousands; there were no arrests. A marcher in London described the atmosphere as "positive, inclusive, and electric."

Speakers at the Washington march included entertainers (Madonna, Ashley Judd, Alicia Keys, America Ferrera), activists in the civil rights struggle (Angela Davis, Tamika Mallory), well-known women who have devoted decades to feminist causes (Gloria Steinem and Planned Parenthood president Cecile Richards), and advocates for immigration reform and LGBT and Native American rights, religious leaders, and filmmaker Michael Moore.

America Ferrera spoke for many when she said, "It's been a heart-rending time to be both a woman and an immigrant this country. Our dignity, our character, our rights have all been under attack, and a platform of hate and division assumed power yesterday."

Gloria Steinem did not hide her scorn of what the new administration represents, inspiring crowds by reminding us all, "Remember, the Constitution doesn't begin with, 'I, the president.' It begins with, 'We, the people.'... To paraphrase a famous quote, I just want to say, I have met the people, and you [Mr. President] are not them."

Citing her organization as part of "the fabric of America for a hundred years," Planned Parenthood's Cecile Richardson exhorted the crowd "to link arms together for the right of working women to earn a living wage, for the right of immigrant families to live without fear, for the right of mothers everywhere... to raise families in safe communities with clean air and clean drinking water, including in Flint, Michigan."

Tamika Mallory spoke bluntly: "Today is not a concert. It is not a parade, and it is not a party. Today is an act of resistance. Now, some of you came here to protest one man. I didn't come here for that. I came here to address those of you who say you are of good conscience."

Madonna was blunter still: "Welcome to the revolution of love," she began, "to the rebellion, to our refusal as women to accept this new age of tyranny, where not just women are in danger, but all marginalized people, where being uniquely different right now might truly be considered a crime." ∎

"NO COUNTRY CAN EVER TRULY FLOURISH IF IT STIFLES THE POTENTIAL OF ITS WOMEN AND DEPRIVES ITSELF OF THE CONTRIBUTIONS OF HALF ITS CITIZENS."
—MICHELLE OBAMA

THE SILENCE
BREAKERS

" "

Human rights are women's rights, and
women's rights are human rights.

—HILLARY CLINTON

TOP: #metoo creator Tarana Burke.

FOLLOWING THE POWERFUL March on Washington in January 2017, major scandals of sexual assault allegations broke throughout Hollywood, snowballing into a massive feminist movement called #metoo. The social media protest #metoo was created in 2006 by Tarana Burke, an activist and founder of a nonprofit that helps survivors of sexual violence, to denounce sexual assault and harassment and encourage women to share their personal experiences. In October 2017, the hashtag went viral after actor Alyssa Milano posted about it on social media and received tens of thousands of replies overnight. The #metoo movement—and subsequent fallout for the accused—swiftly spread around the world, providing solidarity for millions of people to come forward with their stories.

Though this movement appeared seemingly overnight, it had been festering for decades. In the 1970s, most businesses had no procedures for dealing with sexual harassment, and there wasn't even a name for it until a group of women at Cornell University coined the term in 1975.

"The Silence Breakers" were a group of women and men spanning all ages, religions, ethnicities, and industries who came forward about their sexual assault experiences in the workplace. The group was named *Time*'s Person of the Year 2017, and the magazine featured actors Ashley Judd, Rose McGowan, Selma Blair, and Terry Crews; Plaza hotel plaintiffs; State Senator Sara Gelser; musician Taylor Swift; Fox News employees Wendy Walsh and Megyn Kelly; former Uber engineer Susan Fowler; as well as lobbyists, fruit pickers, assistants, dishwashers, and more.

These courageous individuals set aside their own fears of violence, shame, or being fired and spoke out, setting off a shocking chain of events: celebrities, politicians, and business executives were exposed, disgraced, and even fired. Major moments included the firing of Fox News anchor Bill O'Reilly, sexual assault trials against Bill Cosby, and the scandal of producer Harvey Weinstein's nearly 100 assaults.

The Silence Breakers and their worldwide #metoo movement gave people hope that they could and should police sexual assault and inappropriate behavior—and that their voices of protest could facilitate change. ■

IN ORDER FROM LEFT TO RIGHT: **Celebrity Silence Breakers Megyn Kelly, Taylor Swift, Terry Crews, Selma Blair, and Ashley Judd.**

" "

For giving voice to open secrets, for moving whisper networks onto social networks, for pushing us all to stop accepting the unacceptable, the Silence Breakers are the 2017 Person of the Year.

—*TIME* EDITOR-IN-CHIEF EDWARD ELSENTHAL

HOW TO GET INVOLVED

IN THE FIGHT FOR WOMEN'S RIGHTS

RESEARCH · SPEAK OUT · VOLUNTEER
TALK · LISTEN · DONATE · MARCH · VOTE
CALL YOUR LOCAL REPRESENTATIVES
START YOUR OWN ORGANIZATION!

MANY OPPORTUNITIES EXIST to help women and children by volunteering at local institutions that provide shelter, counseling, medical services, legal advice, or mentoring. Positions that require no advanced degrees are available at shelters for women and children, medical clinics that serve women, and social service organizations large enough to have programs focusing on women. Training as a nurse, physician, psychologist, or attorney has obvious value to any helping institution, not just hospitals, but also law offices, centers that support rape victims, victims of domestic violence and abuse, and women who have attempted suicide. Internet skills are also in demand. Contact information can be obtained from an organization's website or Facebook page.

One well-established nonprofit institution that has programs to help women is the U.S. branch of Amnesty International in Washington, DC (amnestyusa.org). Amnesty deals with domestic abuse all over the world. Another nonprofit, the Center for Reproductive Rights

in New York City (reproductiverights.org), is dedicated to supporting women here and abroad in making well-informed decisions about reproductive choices. This legal advocacy organization, which serves many women who seek information to benefit themselves and their families, has joined the ACLU and Planned Parenthood in lawsuits to protect and defend women against restrictive state abortion laws.

Internet-based organizations that have sprung up relatively recently include Hollaback! (ihollaback.org), which works with cities and countries all over the world to educate communities about street harassment and devise solutions that "ensure equal access to public spaces." The local websites and social media pages of SlutWalk explain the mission of this transnational protest movement targeting rape culture. SlutWalk, which originated in Canada, is controversial because the group's signature public activity, the annual march, welcomes nude participants.

VIDA, which works to elevate women in today's literary scene, also collects and shares information about gender gaps in the literary industry and in writers' communities. An ongoing project is the gathering of a dataset that counts and tracks the number of publications by women of color. The volunteers who harvest the data help VIDA generate and present data on gender issues in the literary arts. ■

THE FIGHT FOR RACE RIGHTS

1854
U.S. Congress passes the Kansas-Nebraska Act.

1854
The U.S. Supreme Court rules the Missouri Compromise unconstitutional in the Dred Scott decision.

1861
The Civil War begins.

1863
Abraham Lincoln issues the Emancipation Proclamation.

1896
Plessy v. Ferguson affirms a state's right to regulate intrastate railways, allowing the enforcement of a policy of racial segregation.

1807
U.S. Congress bans the importation of slaves from Africa.

AM I NOT A MAN AND A BROTHER?

1820
U.S. Congress passes the Missouri Compromise.

Ain't I A Woman?

1851
Sojourner Truth gives her "Ain't I a Woman?" speech at a women's rights convention in Ohio.

1859
John Brown commences raid on Harpers Ferry.

1860
The Republican Party chooses Abraham Lincoln as its presidential candidate.

1865
The Civil War ends.

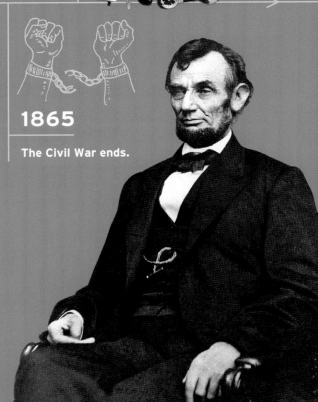

1963

Around 250,000 participants attend the March on Washington for Jobs and Freedom. Dr. Martin Luther King Jr. delivers his "I Have a Dream" speech.

1965

Lyndon B. Johnson signs the Voting Rights Act of 1965.

1965

Malcolm X is assassinated by Nation of Islam members.

1989

Purple Rain protest against Apartheid is held in Cape Town, South Africa.

THE PURPLE SHALL GOVERN!

1989

Bishop Desmond Tutu leads 30,000 marchers in Cape Town peace march.

1995

The Million Man March gathers on Washington.

2014

Civil disturbances and riots break out in Ferguson, Missouri, after Michael Brown is shot dead by police.

BLACK LIVES MATTER

WE WILL NOT FORGET

BLACK LIVES MATTER

WE WILL BE HEARD

The Washington Post
250,000 Jam Mall in Mammoth Rally in Solemn, Orderly Plea for Equality

1955

Rosa Parks is arrested for refusing to give up her bus seat and sparks the thirteen-month-long Montgomery Bus Boycott.

1956

The U.S. Supreme Court declares Alabama law requiring segregation on city buses illegal.

1964

The Civil Rights Act of 1964 bans segregation and outlaws discrimination on the basis of race, color, religion, sex, and national origin.

1968

Dr. Martin Luther King Jr. is assassinated in Memphis, Tennessee.

1991

President George H. W. Bush signs Civil Rights Act of 1991.

1992

Riots erupt in South Central LA after the cops who beat up Rodney King are acquitted.

2009

Barack Obama becomes the first African American U.S. president and the country's forty-fourth president.

2015

South Carolina legislators vote to remove the Confederate flag from the lawn of the statehouse in Charleston.

2017

Confederate monuments are removed from Dallas and New Orleans.

"THE AMERICAN PEOPLE AND THE GOVERNMENT AT WASHINGTON MAY REFUSE TO RECOGNIZE IT FOR A TIME, BUT THE INEXORABLE LOGIC OF EVENTS WILL FORCE IT UPON THEM IN THE END; THAT THE WAR NOW BEING WAGED IN THIS LAND IS A WAR FOR AND AGAINST SLAVERY."

—FREDERICK DOUGLASS

TOP: **Harriet Tubman, late 1870s.**
LEFT: **Black soldier standing guard, 1857.**

U.S. CIVIL WAR

" "

I had reasoned this out in my mind; there was one of two things I had a right to: liberty, or death; if I could not have one, I would have the other.

—HARRIET TUBMAN

THE CIVIL WAR (1861–1865) left a bloody, indelible mark on American history. Militarily, there was brilliant leadership, heroism, and unselfish gallantry on both sides as well as incompetence and cowardice. The behaviors of civilians, which likewise fell along a broad continuum, depended to a large extent on where the individuals happened to live.

In the North, the conflict was officially called the War of the Rebellion. In the South, Confederates used the term "War between the States" and even the "War of Northern Aggression."

In the middle were the areas affected by the tensions between existing pro- and antislavery states. Those came to a head in 1819 when the Missouri territory applied for admission to the Union as a slave state. Intense opposition to this move resulted in an act of Congress known as the Missouri Compromise of 1820: except for its so-called Louisiana Purchase lands, Missouri would become a slave state, and Maine, once a part of Massachusetts, would be free.

The compromise act was repealed in 1854 by the Kansas-Nebraska Act; three years later the Supreme Court

> "THE PROBABILITY
> THAT WE MAY FALL IN
> THE STRUGGLE OUGHT
> NOT TO DETER US
> FROM THE SUPPORT OF
> A CAUSE WE BELIEVE
> TO BE JUST; IT SHALL
> NOT DETER ME."
> —ABRAHAM LINCOLN

confirmed the constitutionality of the repeal in the Dred Scott case. That shameful instance of judicial overreach further declared that, as an African American descended from slaves, Scott, who was living in Illinois, a free state, had no rights as a U.S. citizen, and hence had no standing to sue.

The Dred Scott decision was bookended by the publication of Harriet Beecher Stowe's novel *Uncle Tom's Cabin* in 1852 and by John Brown's 1859 attack on the U.S. arsenal at Harpers Ferry. The Civil War began when the Confederates fired on Fort Sumter, tenuously held by the Union despite the recent secession of South Carolina.

The Thirteenth Amendment, which abolished slavery in the United States, was ratified in 1865. Then came the Reconstruction period, which saw many advances for blacks in civic life, business, and politics. However, soon Reconstruction was replaced by

the seventy-four-year-long Jim Crow period. It was a time of persecution of blacks ranging from lynchings by private citizens to legalized segregation in many parts of the country, mainly the South. This period is said to have ended in 1954 with the Supreme Court's decision declaring school desegregation illegal, but implementation was slow and some would argue segregation still continues today. The Civil Rights Act of 1964 put teeth into the Fourteenth Amendment of 1868 (specifying that U.S. citizens have civil rights, including due process) and the Fifteenth Amendment of 1870, section 1 of which states: "The right of citizens of the United States to vote shall not be denied or abridged by the United States or by any state on account of race, color, or previous condition of servitude." ■

LEFT: **Wood cut of a popular symbol for abolitionists, adopted as the seal of the Society for the Abolition of Slavery in England in the 1780s.**

ABOLITION
OF SLAVERY

" "

If there is no struggle, there is no progress. Those who profess to favor freedom, and yet depreciate agitation, are men who want crops without plowing up the ground.

—FREDERICK DOUGLASS

OPPOSITION TO SLAVERY in the West dates back to the lonely efforts of Granville Sharp, an English lawyer who spoke out against his country's legalization of the practice. In 1772, he assisted in the winning defense of an American slave, James Somerset. Granville's strategy resulted in a change in law: "as soon as any slave sets foot upon English territory, he becomes free."

However, the Somerset decision was not applicable in the American colonies, and in 1833 the American Anti-Slavery Society (AAS) was founded in Philadelphia, becoming a leader in the fight for emancipation of slaves in the United States. Controversial and often provoking violent opposition, the AAS was led by men such as William Lloyd Garrison, editor of the outspoken antislavery journal the *Liberator*, and fiery orator Frederick Douglass, who had bought his own freedom.

Isabella Baumfree, known to history as Sojourner Truth, was born a slave. As a free woman, she was a leading activist in the fight to end slavery and in efforts to assist others to escape from states

TOP: **Abraham Lincoln showing Sojourner Truth the Bible, 1864.**
BOTTOM: **Frederick Douglass, 1870.**

where slavery was legal. Sojourner Truth delivered her famous "Ain't I a Woman?" speech in 1851 at a women's rights convention in Ohio.

More conservative abolitionists came to the forefront of the movement in the 1840s and 1850s; the Republican Party, formed in 1854, chose Abraham Lincoln as its presidential candidate in 1860 and 1864. Lincoln's Emancipation Proclamation of 1863, while it by no means completed the struggle, remains its foundational document.

Later in the nineteenth century, the inhumane doctrine of "separate but equal" became the law of the land in the infamous Supreme Court case of *Plessy v. Ferguson*. Twentieth-century decisions, beginning with *Brown v. Board of Education*, supplemented by the Civil Rights Act of 1964 and related legislation, have done much to overcome the legacy of slavery in this country.

Advances in civil rights law nevertheless fell short of benefiting all African Americans, and young people of all races—for various reasons—adopted the slogan "Power to the People."

The illegality of buying, enslaving, and selling black people is firmly established in the United States. Human trafficking, a crime that has victimized mainly women and children, remains an injustice to be eradicated. ■

RIGHT: Union general R. H. Milroy's notice of the Emancipation Proclamation to the citizens of Winchester, Virginia.

FREEDOM TO SLAVES!

Whereas, the President of the United States did, on the first day of the present month, issue his *Proclamation* declaring "that *all persons held as Slaves in certain designated States, and parts of States, are, and henceforward shall be free,*" and that the Executive Government of the United States, including the Military and Naval authorities thereof, would recognize and maintain the freedom of said persons. *And Whereas,* the county of *Frederick* is included in the territory designated by the Proclamation of the President, in which the *Slaves should become free,* I therefore hereby notify the citizens of the city of Winchester, and of said County, of said Proclamation, and of my intention to maintain and enforce the same.

I expect all citizens to yield a ready compliance with the Proclamation of the Chief Executive, and I admonish all persons disposed to resist its peaceful enforcement, that upon manifesting such disposition by acts, they will be regarded as rebels in arms against the lawful authority of the Federal Government and dealt with accordingly.

All persons liberated by said Proclamation are admonished to abstain from all violence, and immediately betake themselves to useful occupations.

The officers of this command are admonished and ordered to act in accordance with said proclamation and to yield their ready co-operation in its enforcement.

R. H. Milroy,
Brig. Gen'l Commanding.

Jan. 5th, 1863.

SEPARATE BUT EQUAL:
1955 MONTGOMERY BUS BOYCOTT

" "

In this country, "American" means "white."
Everybody else has to hyphenate.

—TONI MORRISON

TOP: **Leaders of the Montgomery boycott wait for a bus, 1956.**
BOTTOM: **Two white women sit in an otherwise empty bus, 1956.**

THE JIM CROW period gave rise to another phrase that was adopted by segregationist Americans to designate and rationalize segregation, injustices and all. "Separate but equal" is a reordered, perhaps milder-sounding, version of "equal but separate," the operative term of a Louisiana law of 1890.

The Louisiana law was later invoked in an 1896 Supreme Court case. Four years earlier, a black man named Homer Plessy had been arrested for disobeying a railroad employee's request that he give up his seat on a train to a white person, in accordance with the law. The arrest was not a surprise, for Plessy had agreed to become the plaintiff in a test case aimed at nullifying the unpopular statute.

Plessy v. Ferguson arrived at the Supreme Court after lower court judges had affirmed the right of Louisiana to regulate railway companies within state boundaries. (John Ferguson was the first Louisiana judge to so rule.) The Supreme Court justice who delivered the Court's opinion was a patrician native New Englander named Henry B. Brown. In an opinion that has been vigorously criticized ever since, Justice Brown rejected arguments citing the Thirteenth and Fourteenth Amendments and opined that laws could not overcome "social prejudices" and "that equal rights cannot be secured to the negro except by an enforced commingling of the two races." The sole dissenter, Justice John Marshall

Harlan, noted that "our Constitution is color-blind" and deemed "the arbitrary separation of citizens [on a public highway] on the basis of race" unconstitutional.

Another citizen on a public highway, Rosa Parks, famously resisted being separated from her fellow citizens on the basis of race. On December 5, 1955, when a bus driver ordered her and two other black residents of Montgomery, Alabama, to move to the back of the bus, two passengers complied. Mrs. Parks said, "No." When told that she'd be arrested, she answered quietly, "You may do that." The police came, made the arrest, and issued a fine of ten dollars.

What happened next is equally well known. The Montgomery Improvement Association (MIA), led by a thirty-six-year-old pastor, Dr. Martin Luther King Jr., organized a boycott of Montgomery's buses until black passengers were treated fairly and courteously. The nonviolent action

lasted thirteen months, during which almost all black residents walked or used bicycles; carpools were arranged for the elderly. The bus company lost thousands of dollars. Dr. King and Ralph Abernathy, with whom he had cofounded the Southern Christian Leadership Conference (SCLC), were arrested, and their homes were bombed, along with four churches. Slowly, *Browder v. Gayle* worked its way through state courts in an attempt to vindicate Aurelia Browder and three other black women who had been mistreated on city buses; William Gayle was Montgomery's mayor. On December 17, 1956, the Supreme Court ruled the state law requiring segregation on city buses unconstitutional. Three days later, Dr. King and the MIA voted to end the protest.

As Rosa Parks said, "People always say that I didn't give up my seat because I was tired, but that isn't true. I was not tired physically... No, the only tired I was, was tired of giving in." ■

The Power of Protest

TOP: **Malcolm X, 1964.**
BOTTOM: **Folk singer Joan Baez and novelist and critic James Baldwin attend the Selma civil rights march.**

CIVIL RIGHTS
MOVEMENT, 1960s

" "

We can never get civil rights in America until our human rights are first restored. We will never be recognized as citizens there until we are first recognized as humans.

—MALCOLM X

IN THE DECADES between the post–Civil War Reconstruction period (1865–1877), when black Americans were introduced to many of the rights other Americans took for granted, and the Civil Rights Movement of the 1960s, those rights were snatched away by restrictive legislation and local ordinances. The Jim Crow era, which followed Reconstruction, was one of rigid segregation and routine—potentially fatal—denials of due process and equal protection. It was time for a major push for African American civil rights.

In the wake of such earlier protests as the Montgomery Bus Boycott, others appalled by the treatment of their fellow citizens became pushers too. They were mainly white, middle-class students or educated adults; many were clergy or religious individuals.

Although segregation in public schools had been outlawed in 1954 by the Supreme Court's ruling in *Brown v. Board of Education*, integration did not begin to be achieved until 1957, when President Eisenhower ordered the Arkansas National Guard to protect nine

ABOVE: **Three demonstrators join hands to build strength against the force of water sprayed by riot police in Birmingham, Alabama.**

ABOVE: **Dr. Martin Luther King Jr. and his wife, Coretta Scott King, lead the Selma to Montgomery voting rights march.**

students who were eligible to attend an integrated school, Little Rock Central High School. Even when the Guard troops were fortified by members of the elite 101st Airborne Division, Little Rock residents jeered and spat at the students as they entered the school; their classmates were verbally abusive and attacked the newcomers physically when out of sight of the soldiers.

Beginning with the lunch counter sit-ins of 1958-1960, protests became more confrontational. The first innovation of the 1960s was the Freedom Rides through the Deep South, where activists rode buses to test a recent Supreme Court ruling that banned segregation of passengers engaged in interstate travel. Protesters encountered violence and threats in Alabama, where one bus was firebombed, endangering everyone aboard. Arrests occurred throughout the South, and those who were jailed in tiny, filthy cells were often beaten. These activists were young, representing organizations including the Congress on Racial Equality (CORE) and the Student Nonviolent Coordinating Committee (SNCC).

The protests drew the attention of President John F. Kennedy, who in 1961 had the Interstate Commerce Commission issue a desegregation order containing specifics: no more "white" and "colored" signs; consolidation of services like drinking fountains, toilets, and waiting rooms; lunch counters to serve anyone who cared to patronize them.

Next, representatives of the National Association for the Advancement of Colored People (NAACP), CORE, SNCC, and the Southern Christian Leadership Conference turned to the essential issue of voter registration, as many black people in the South had been illegally prevented from registering, and others didn't think it wise to even try. While these protests impressed members of Congress who would later vote for the Civil Right Act of 1964 and the Voting Rights Act of 1965, they were overshadowed in 1963 by the March on Washington for Jobs and Freedom. Indeed, that civil rights landmark is often called the catalyst that led to the passage, within a year, of the Civil Rights Act. ■

"FROM MY POINT OF VIEW, NO LABEL, NO SLOGAN, NO PARTY, NO SKIN COLOR, AND INDEED NO RELIGION IS MORE IMPORTANT THAN THE HUMAN BEING."
—JAMES BALDWIN

MARCH ON WASHINGTON, 1963

" "

I have a dream...I say to you today, my friends, that in spite of the difficulties and frustrations of the moment, I still have a dream.

—DR. MARTIN LUTHER KING JR.

TOP: **A. Philip Randolph and other civil rights leaders on their way to Congress during the March on Washington, 1963.**
BOTTOM: **Marchers carrying signs for equal rights, integrated schools, and decent housing.**
LEFT: **Dr. Martin Luther King Jr. and other civil rights leaders meet JFK.**

IT WAS DR. KING whose "I Have a Dream" speech galvanized a quarter-million people in front of the Lincoln Memorial on that August day; but the organizers of the march were also giants in the long-running struggle for civil rights. They were labor leaders Bayard Rustin and A. Philip Randolph. Rustin, who held radical political views, believed in nonviolence and was one of the founders of the SCLC; he was doubly discriminated against all his life because he was gay as well as black. Randolph, whose agitation at the outset of World War II had helped persuade President Franklin D. Roosevelt to outlaw employment discrimination in the defense industry, was the founder and first president of the Brotherhood of Sleeping Car Porters.

The March on Washington is always cited as the crowning popular achievement of the Civil Rights Movement in the 1960s, and in 1964 Dr. King was awarded the Nobel Peace Prize. However, violence was never completely absent, often at the hands of southern opponents of the increased inclusion of blacks on the

Dr. Martin Luther King Jr. addressing the crowd of demonstrators outside the Lincoln Memorial.

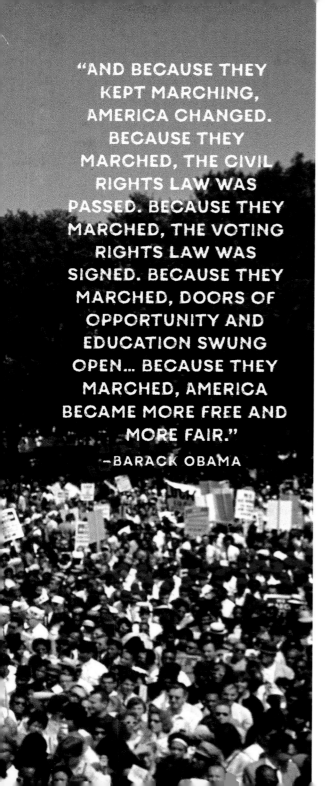

"AND BECAUSE THEY KEPT MARCHING, AMERICA CHANGED. BECAUSE THEY MARCHED, THE CIVIL RIGHTS LAW WAS PASSED. BECAUSE THEY MARCHED, THE VOTING RIGHTS LAW WAS SIGNED. BECAUSE THEY MARCHED, DOORS OF OPPORTUNITY AND EDUCATION SWUNG OPEN... BECAUSE THEY MARCHED, AMERICA BECAME MORE FREE AND MORE FAIR."
—BARACK OBAMA

voter rolls. An SNCC voter registration program in Selma was forcefully opposed by Sheriff Jim Clark. People continued to march, and the death of a protester in 1965 brought together leaders of SNCC and the SCLC, who planned a march from Selma to the capital, Montgomery, a distance of fifty-four miles.

Participants in the event universally report feelings of uplift, brotherhood and sisterhood, empowerment, and hope. A sense of optimism prevailed over the coming two years, which would see the passage of the Civil Rights Act of 1964 and the Voting Rights Act of 1965. Desegregation of the public schools was proceeding, albeit slowly. The goodwill generated by the peaceful gathering of more than 200,000 people may have dissipated in some quarters, but periodically, often in response to troubled times, Americans remember their experience of the march, whether personal or vicarious, and summon the will to continue.

Surely the most remembered part of the program offered to the vast audience on the National Mall was King's "I Have a Dream" speech, carried by radio and live TV to tens of millions. But there were other speakers: the march organizers, Bayard Rustin and the Reverend Ralph David Abernathy, NAACP leader Roy Wilkins, and John Lewis, then of the Student Nonviolent Coordinating Committee, who as of 2017 is representing Georgia's Fifth Congressional District in Washington.

Musicians beloved in the black community, including Mahalia Jackson, Odetta, and the Freedom Singers, performed. Jackson's emotionally and physically charged performance of the gospel classic "How I Got Over" had people dancing and crying at the same time. An underlying concern over "white co-optation" surfaced in connection with the number of white performers, despite their well-known support of civil rights causes. But the crowd joined in readily when Joan Baez led them in "We Shall Overcome." Bob Dylan sang "Only a Pawn in Their Game," about the murder of Medgar Evers. He also introduced a song he had not released yet, "The Times They Are A-Changin'."

Unlike many benefits and demonstrations today, the March on Washington drew relatively few celebrities, and their sincerity was undoubted. UN diplomat and Nobel laureate Dr. Ralph Bunche was there, as was writer James Baldwin, a longtime resident of France owing to disillusionment with the racism he had endured as a young man. Actors Sidney Poitier, Harry Belafonte, Ossie Davis, Charlton Heston, and Marlon Brando quietly graced the scene. Jackie Robinson, who broke baseball's color line when he joined the Brooklyn Dodgers in 1947, was there, along with a younger athletic star, the Celtics's Bill Russell.

Uncertain of the reception he might receive, the president, John F. Kennedy, did not attend the march but met with the leaders in the Oval Office. On the fiftieth anniversary of the march, the nation's first black president, Barack Obama, delivered a moving speech at the Lincoln Memorial. ■

RIGHT: **Massive crowd assembled in Washington, DC, to hear Dr. Martin Luther King Jr. deliver his "I Have a Dream" speech.**

The Power of Protest

PURPLE RAIN PROTEST
IN CAPE TOWN

" "

I am not interested in picking up crumbs of compassion thrown from the table of someone who considers himself my master. I want the full menu of human rights.

—ARCHBISHOP DESMOND TUTU

TOP: **Archbishop Desmond Tutu, 2009.**
BOTTOM: **Students gather outside a school in Johannesburg to protest racially segregated hospitals, 1989.**

THE PURPLE RAIN protest in Cape Town, South Africa, was among the twentieth century's most spectacular demonstrations of popular opposition to racial discrimination. It was surely the most colorful. News media all over the world picked up local footage of police water cannons spraying purple water at the protesters. The water had been dyed because many arrests were anticipated, and the purple skin and clothing of the protesters, many of whom had traveled from elsewhere in South Africa, would facilitate identification.

In 1989, the long-simmering anti-Apartheid movement in South Africa was within a few years of victory, but the government of President P. W. Botha, known by the outlawed African National Congress and its supporters of all races as "the great crocodile," showed no sign of coming to terms with those who wanted an end to the government's policy of strict racial segregation. Accordingly, the Mass Democratic Movement, a loose association of nonracial anti-Apartheid groups, had been planning a march in Cape Town for

> "I was born a crime. I was born to a black South African mother and a white Swiss father during Apartheid in South Africa, and them [having sex] was illegal. Apartheid only ended in 1990, so for the first six years of my life, I was just living this life of being a physical crime."
>
> —TREVOR NOAH

September 2, 1989, four days before a parliamentary election.

The marchers were accorded a harsh reception. Riot police manned the water cannon, wielded whips and batons, discharged tear gas, and used attack dogs. However, at a critical moment the officer training the hose on the marchers lost control of the nozzle—a protester had grabbed it and turned it on nearby office buildings, including the headquarters of the ruling National Party.

Botha, as it happens, had resigned only days before. He was succeeded by F. W. de Klerk, who in 1994, with great goodwill, would turn the presidency over to Nelson Mandela. In September 1989, de Klerk quickly took charge of the situation and approved a permit for another march a few days later.

Thirty thousand people joined Anglican bishop Desmond Tutu on that march. Coincidentally, the bishop wore purple, the color appropriate to that period in the church calendar.

The march on Cape Town united people from across the spectrum of anti-Apartheid activists. They included Helen Joseph, a white woman who had been an organizer of the earlier march on Pretoria (see page 49); Sister Mary Bernard Ncuba, an often-arrested Roman Catholic nun; Bishop Tutu; Dr. Allan Boesak, who later was a corecipient of the Human Rights Award of the Robert F. Kennedy Center for Justice and Human Rights; and attorney Essa Moosa, who had defended political detainees and, after the end of Apartheid, was a judge on the Supreme Court of South Africa. ■

ABOVE: **Cape Town protester redirects a water cannon into nearby office buildings.**

RACE RELATIONS
IN THE '70s, '80s, '90s

66 99

The problem is, first of all, the police are trained to win no matter what. Win an argument, win a situation—that's how they're taught. You add racism to that and it's just an evil combination.

—ICE CUBE

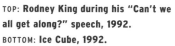

TOP: **Rodney King during his "Can't we all get along?" speech, 1992.**
BOTTOM: **Ice Cube, 1992.**

THE DECADES BETWEEN 1970 and the new millennium saw some solid gains for African Americans and other ethnic minorities, but the scope of the civil rights acts of the mid-1960s remained unsurpassed. In fact, there were setbacks in race relations, and progress often was made not in Congress or the courts but in popular culture.

U.S. labor laws had long needed strengthening to discourage and punish employment discrimination. Title VII of the Civil Rights Act of 1964 updated the Civil Rights Act of 1866, which addressed Reconstruction-era conditions without attempting to speculate about society's requirements a century later. For example, the 1991 act strengthened the 1964 law's provisions relating to race-based harassment on the job and its disparate impact. The new law, signed by President George H. W. Bush, represented a compromise between a 1990 act covering the same ground with additional protections for plaintiffs, which Bush had vetoed.

Race relations took a distinct downturn in 1992 when South-Central

Los Angeles was shaken by five days of rioting after a jury acquitted four white police officers for beating a black cab driver, Rodney King. The incident had been videotaped by a witness who sent his footage to a local TV channel. King's injuries included eleven fractures.

The riots left more than 50 people dead and more than 2,000 injured; estimated cost of damages to more than a thousand buildings in the area exceeded $1 billion. Order was restored by California National Guard troops. The Rodney King riots helped bring recognition to poor U.S. race relations on an international scale.

Rodney King's ordeal was seen by many as an overreaction by police due to racial profiling, the assumption that an individual's race, ethnicity, religion, or national origin was grounds for suspicion of criminality. Blacks, Latinos, and Asian Americans were the primary targets of profiling in the 1980s and '90s, long before the Rodney King riots. The Civil Rights Act of 1991 helped to some extent: once harassment in the workplace could be litigated.

In this unpromising social environment, hip-hop, the cultural phenomenon born in the 1970s, became a vocal outlet for those feeling attacked.

In fact, despite problems involving citations for obscenity, which affected record store salesmen as well as artists, the genre continued to thrive and find a place in U.S. culture like never before. While there were criticisms from those who believed hip-hop promoted drug use, misogyny, violence, and criminality, songs such as N.W.A's 1988 hit, "Fuck Tha Police" remained popular—an anthem to a movement that would continue to impact the 90s, early 2000s, and beyond. ■

MILLION MAN
MARCH

" "

We will march on so over-aggressive law enforcement procedures will not be the order of the day. We will march on until every child has access to high-quality education. We will march so that every citizen will know that they can get health care.

—DANNY K. DAVIS

TOP AND BOTTOM: **Protesters gather for the Million Man March, 1995.**
LEFT: **Rioters in downtown LA after officers were cleared of all charges in the Rodney King case, 1992.**

THE GATHERING OF African American men in Washington, DC, known as the Million Man March, filled the National Mall and surrounding areas on October 16, 1995. Crowd size numbers varied, but even the low estimate (400,000 by the U.S. Park Police) was far higher than previous turnouts by that population. In addition, controversies associated with the leader of the march, Nation of Islam head Louis Farrakhan, tended to obscure both the context and the purpose of the event.

In anticipation of the 1996 presidential election, civil rights activists all over the country wanted to mount grassroots voter registration campaigns that would draw politicians' attention to issues affecting minorities and poor city dwellers. The march, which did not focus on any particular tactic for enhancing civil rights, was intended to give the lie to racist stereotypes about black men. It was hoped that those who attended would come away encouraged to work together to improve their communities in the face of daunting economic and social problems.

The decision to exclude women from the march (though a few did participate) was an issue for many. Therefore, women organized an event on the same day: the Day of Absence. Because travel expenses ruled out participation for men with low-paying jobs, the plan for the Day of Absence was for all black Americans to abstain from work, school, and social engagements, instead attending teach-ins and worship services that would consider paths to a healthier, more self-sufficient black community.

The speakers at the march addressed the themes of atonement, reconciliation, and responsibility, often from a religious standpoint. The religions represented were Islam and Protestant Christianity; indigenous African culture was honored with performances by drummers and dancers. The speakers themselves were religious leaders and thinkers, elected politicians, women who had inspired millions, and relatives of revered African American leaders. The long list included Farrakhan himself; Benjamin Chavis, the organizer of the march and former executive director of the NAACP; Betty Shabazz, the widow of Malcolm X; Dr. Martin Luther King III; Rosa Parks; Maya Angelou; Jeremiah Wright, then pastor of the Chicago church attended by Barack and Michelle Obama; Cornel West; and Jesse Jackson.

The organizers, program participants, and attendees saw the event as a great success, but enthusiasm was restrained in some quarters. The NAACP withheld its support from the march, but individual chapters could make their own decisions. The Chicago chapter set a goal of 47,000 men; the New York chapter hoped to send 250,000. The *Washington Post* and the *New York Times* ran dueling op-eds. The local paper's journalist called Farrakhan's speech both "striking" and "a stemwinder."

Farrakhan organized another march in the twentieth-anniversary year of the Million Man March. It was held on October 20, 2015. ■

LEFT: **Thousands gather outside of the U.S. Capitol building.**
RIGHT: **Hands raise in a show of unity during the Million Man March.**

The Power of Protest

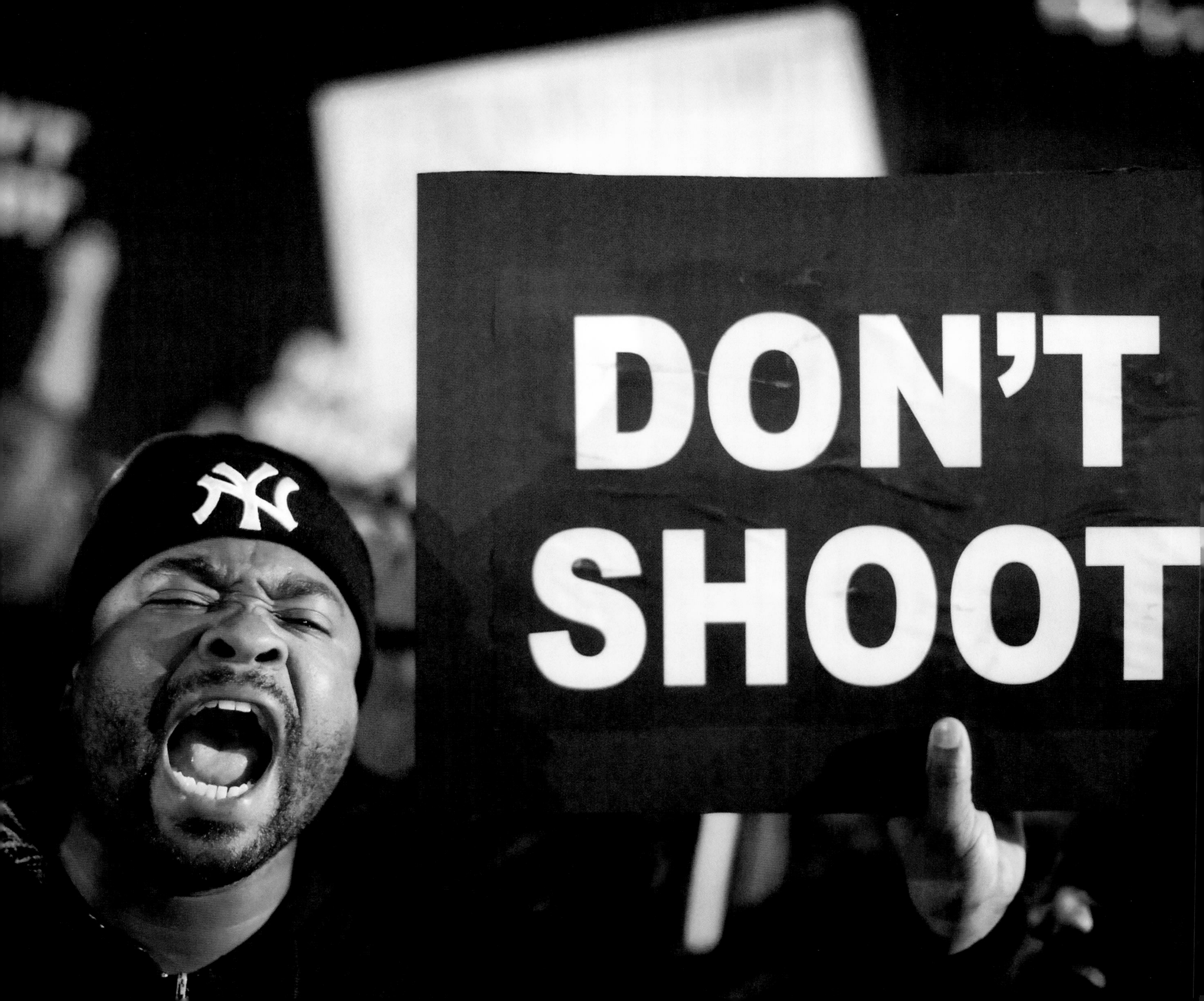
DON'T
SHOOT

BLACK LIVES MATTER

" "

The only reason you say that race was not an issue is because you wish it was not. We all wish it was not. But it's a lie. I came from a country where race was not an issue; I did not think of myself as black and I only became black when I came to America.

—CHIMAMANDA NGOZI ADICHIE

BLACK LIVES MATTER

TOP: **Protesters in New York City march in solidarity with Ferguson, MO.**
BOTTOM: **Ferguson, MO, demonstrators protest the shooting of teenager Michael Brown by an officer.**
LEFT: **Protesters march through the streets of St. Louis, MO, after the killing of Vonderrit Myers Jr. by an officer.**

BLACK LIVES MATTER (BLM) was born in July 2013, after the news broke that George Zimmerman, the man charged with the murder of seventeen-year-old Trayvon Martin, was acquitted on grounds of self-defense. Within hours, Alicia Garza, a saddened Californian, had put up a Facebook post ending with "Black people, I love you, I love us. Our lives matter." One of Alicia Garza's friends, a community organizer named Patrisse Cullors, read the post and responded, using the hashtag #blacklivesmatter. The two women,

joined by Opal Tometi, an immigrant-rights activist, set up Twitter and Tumblr accounts in that name. Around the same time, Cullors led a march down Rodeo Drive in Beverly Hills, behind a banner carrying the hashtag.

Barely a year later, in Ferguson, Missouri, Michael Brown, nineteen years old and unarmed, was shot dead in an altercation with a white police officer. The next day, August 10, 2014, protests accompanied by acts of vandalism and looting brought police in riot gear into the streets. Garza, Cullors, and

Tometi organized a "freedom ride" to Ferguson, and hundreds of people from all over the country signed up to participate. Garza was surprised to hear the protesting Ferguson residents shouting "Black lives matter!" and carrying the hashtag signs.

The slogan and the movement continued to gain traction when a grand jury declined to indict Ferguson police officer Darren Wilson for Brown's death. Wilson, having recognized Brown and another man from descriptions of suspects in a recent robbery, had blocked the men with his cruiser. Brown attempted to wrest Wilson's firearm from him through the car window and, in the struggle, was fatally shot.

As the death toll of unarmed black males continued to climb, protests under the banner of #blacklivesmatter mounted. On November 22, 2014, twelve-year-old Tamir Rice was shot by Cleveland police officers who said they had thought his replica handgun was an actual firearm. Soon after, Hillary Clinton used "black lives matter" in a speech at a human rights gala. It was apparent that despite the election and reelection of a black president, African Americans remained at a disadvantage in many areas, including education,

LEFT: **Protesters march with their mouths covered by tape reading "I Can't Breathe" in Miami, FL.**
RIGHT: **Marchers in the Journey for Justice, a 120-mile march from the apartments where Michael Brown was shot to the Governor's mansion in Jefferson City, MO.**

housing, and an unjustly high rate of incarceration.

Unlike the Civil Rights struggle of the '50s and '60s, with its high-profile charismatic leaders like Dr. Martin Luther King Jr. and Malcolm X, the democratic BLM movement is not guided by any single man. In fact, many of its leaders are women and LGBT activists. Garza, who identifies as queer, is married to a transgender man. Bowdoin graduate DeRay Mckesson, with his hundreds of thousands of Twitter followers, is a gay man who tweeted reports of confrontations on the streets of Ferguson in the period following Brown's death. In March 2017 there were thirty-seven Black Lives Matter chapters across the United States and one in Canada.

The guiding principles of Black Lives Matter are summarized on the organization's website: "Black Lives Matter is an ideological and political intervention in a world where Black lives are systematically and intentionally targeted for demise. It is an affirmation of Black folks' contributions to this society, our humanity, and our resilience in the face of deadly oppression."

The group, as part of the "global Black family," acknowledges that the experience of American blacks is unique in the global family as to privilege and as to impact. Its members are "committed to disrupting the Western-prescribed nuclear family structure requirement by supporting each other as extended families and 'villages' that collectively care for one another, and especially 'our' children, to the degree that mothers, parents, and children are comfortable."

A central value of BLM is stated as follows: "all Black lives [matter], regardless of actual or perceived sexual identity, gender identity, gender expression, economic status, ability, disability, religious beliefs or disbeliefs, immigration status or location. The goal of restorative justice is to be achieved by working courageously [and] vigorously for freedom and justice for Black people and, by extension, all people."

Reception of BLM in the community at large has been mixed. People with decades of civil rights work behind them are sometimes put off by the group's confrontational tactics. They point to earlier activists who, like Rosa Parks in 1955, reacted to racist injustice with quiet dignity. More recently, the relatives of slain participants in the Bible study class at Emanuel African Methodist Episcopal Church in Charleston, South Carolina, were restrained, often forgiving, when asked to comment on the confessed shooter, twenty-one-year-old Dylann Roof.

Not long after the church murders in June 2015, BLM activist Bree Newsome climbed a flagpole in front of the statehouse in Charleston and pulled down the Confederate flag. A month later, the state legislature voted to bring down the flag permanently and officially. ■

HOW TO GET INVOLVED

IN THE FIGHT FOR RACE RIGHTS

RESEARCH • SPEAK OUT • VOLUNTEER
TALK • LISTEN • DONATE • MARCH • VOTE
CALL YOUR LOCAL REPRESENTATIVES
START YOUR OWN ORGANIZATION!

OPPORTUNITIES TO GET involved in the fight for race rights are so numerous that once committed, some find themselves overwhelmed with volunteering, marching, leafleting, and knocking on doors, reading every petition that hits their inboxes, and helping out financially whenever possible. However, when high initial enthusiasm leads to early burnout, it's a loss for all concerned.

The struggle is neither new nor small in scope, and it is likely to remain active for years to come. A plan is helpful for those who wish to get involved. Many people start by attending meetings with a friend who already belongs to a rights group. If this doesn't work for you, there are scores of national organizations with branches in hundreds of cities. These range from the venerable NAACP (founded in 1909) to the confrontational Black Lives Matter. Smaller groups form, often under the auspices of a house of worship or by the efforts of relatives, in response to local issues that have a short half-life in the national news.

Organizations to contact are easy to find on the internet. One comprehensive source is startguide.org.

This resource provides names of groups devoted to civil rights, like Race Forward, and constituency groups focusing on African American issues like the Urban League, the National Council of Negro Women, and the A. Philip Randolph Institute. Also listed are the National Council of American Indians, the National Council of La Raza, and organizations that work for Asian Americans.

Legal defense organizations include the NAACP Legal Defense Fund, the Southern Poverty Law Center, and the Brennan Center for Justice. It isn't necessary to be an attorney or paralegal to be useful to these organizations.

Additional groups work another aspect of legal defense: criminal justice. The Innocence Project and the Justice Project—Campaign for Criminal Justice Reform address not only areas in which the American criminal justice system needs reform but inaccuracies in that system, such as eyewitness misidentification. The mission statement of the Prison Policy Initiative describes its work as producing "cutting-edge research to expose the broader harm of mass criminalization" and encouraging advocacy campaigns designed to lead to a more just society.

Most of these organizations welcome assistance in fund-raising and publicizing new or ongoing initiatives. Specialized training is always helpful, but daycare centers in urban areas, providers of after-school tutoring, Big Brother/Sister Programs, and local groups that assist housebound or disabled people will be glad to help volunteers learn the ropes. Notices in laundromats and bodegas may lead you to a student who needs you. If you have psychology training or are a veteran of a twelve-step group, you can inquire about volunteer opportunities at homeless shelters and substance abuse programs run by municipalities. The opportunities for service are abundant. ■

THE FIGHT FOR GAY RIGHTS

The Stonewall Inn

1969

The Stonewall Inn, in New York's Greenwich Village, becomes the scene of a days-long riot to protest discriminatory treatment by the police.

1978

Gilbert Baker designs and flies the first rainbow flag at the San Francisco Pride parade.

GAY IS GOOD

1982

Wisconsin becomes the first state to outlaw discrimination based on sexual orientation.

mattachine recommends me

WE HOMOSEXUALS PLEAD WITH OUR PEOPLE TO PLEASE HELP MAINTAIN PEACEFUL AND QUIET CONDUCT ON THE STREETS OF THE VILLAGE — MATTACHINE

1950

The Mattachine Society, one of the United States' oldest gay rights groups, forms in Los Angeles.

1961

Illinois becomes the first state to decriminalize sodomy between consenting partners.

1973

The American Psychiatric Association removes homosexuality from its list of mental disorders.

Homosexuality is not a mental disorder and thus there is no need for a cure.
— AMERICAN PSYCHOLOGICAL ASSOCIATION

SILENCE=DEATH

1981

Writer Larry Kramer hosts a meeting that results in the formation of the Gay Men's Health Crisis, which began to offer services for the prevention and cure of AIDS.

1989–1996

Denmark, followed by Norway, Sweden, Greenland, and Iceland, recognizes registered partnerships.

LOVE IS LOVE

1999

The Transgender Day of Remembrance is founded in the United States, and then later in the UK and worldwide.

2004

The first legal same-sex marriage in the United States takes place in Massachusetts.

2012

Tammy Baldwin becomes the first openly gay politician and the first Wisconsin woman to be elected to the U.S. Senate.

2016

President Barack Obama dedicates the Stonewall National Monument near the site of the original bar.

1996

Hawaii rules that the state does not have a legal right to deprive same-sex couples of the right to marry, making Hawaii the first state to recognize that gay and lesbian couples are entitled to the same privileges as heterosexual married couples.

2003

In *Lawrence v. Texas*, the U.S. Supreme Court declares unconstitutional laws criminalizing same-sex activity, in private, between consenting adults.

2011

The U.S. military policy of "Don't Ask, Don't Tell" is officially decertified.

2015

The U.S. Supreme Court ruling in *Obergefell v. Hodges* legalizes same-sex marriage in the United States.

2017

Turing's Law posthumously pardons thousands convicted of now-abolished sexual offenses in Britain.

2017

District of Columbia residents can choose a gender-neutral option for their driver's license.

2018

The U.S. Military signs service contract with the first openly transgender person to be accepted into the army after the ban on transgender personnel is lifted.

Transgender day of Remembrance

LOVE WINS

RESIST

"THE STONEWALL UPRISING...IS TO THE GAY MOVEMENT WHAT THE FALL OF THE BASTILLE IS TO THE UNLEASHING OF THE FRENCH REVOLUTION."
—DAVID CARTER

STONEWALL
AND THE MOVEMENT THAT FOLLOWED

❝ ❞

It takes no compromise to give people their rights...it takes no money to respect the individual. It takes no political deal to give people freedom. It takes no survey to remove repression.

—HARVEY MILK

TOP: **Harvey Milk, the first openly gay elected official in the history of California, 1978.**
BOTTOM: **Sylvia Rivera, Stonewall veteran, activist, and founding member of the Gay Liberation Front, the Street Transvestite Action Revolutionaries (STAR), and the Gay Activists Alliance, 1994.**
LEFT: **A crowd marches in New York in the first Gay Pride march, held one month after the Stonewall Inn riot, 1969.**

FIFTY YEARS AGO, the gay rights movement was brewing in New York and other large American cities, but repressive, highly discriminatory local ordinances were in still effect; police harassment of patrons of gay bars was commonplace. Harassment was particularly commonplace on Christopher Street in Greenwich Village, where many gays and lesbians lived and gathered in bars like the Stonewall Inn. Other Stonewall regulars were transgender women of color, who received special attention when police raided their hangout.

Before the events today known collectively as the Stonewall riots, serving alcohol to gays was illegal in New York City; gays caught dancing with each other could be arrested. In the repressive antiminority atmosphere of the time, the police routinely entered gay bars because they could; bar employees and owners could do little to challenge them. The mafia owned many gay bars in the city, including the Stonewall, a factor that complicated the situation with respect to liquor licenses and health code violations.

"

All of us who are openly gay are living and writing the history of our movement. We are no more—and no less—heroic than the suffragists and abolitionists of the nineteenth century, and the labor organizers, Freedom Riders, Stonewall demonstrators, and environmentalists of the twentieth century. We are ordinary people, living our lives, and trying, as civil rights activist Dorothy Cotton said, to "fix what ain't right" in our society.

—SENATOR TAMMY BALDWIN

At 1:20 a.m. on June 28, 1969, NYPD officers raided the Stonewall Inn; the 200 or so patrons outnumbered them roughly twenty-five to one. The police proceeded to arrest bar employees for selling liquor without a license, and officers began to physically harass patrons. They also arrested several women who were not wearing at least three articles of gender-appropriate clothing, citing a city criminal statute.

Before the first patrol wagon arrived, about 150 people had assembled, and the crowd kept growing. A lesbian who had scuffled with the policemen escorting her to the patrol wagon complained that her handcuffs were too tight. She was hit in the head, then picked up and thrown into the vehicle. Her reported remonstrance to the crowd, "Why don't you guys do something?" was the spark that ignited the first night's rioting. It began with jeers and thrown objects—pennies, bottles, rocks, garbage cans. Soon the bar was set afire, the fire was extinguished, and officers from the raid, having called for backup, had barricaded themselves inside the bar. By 4:00 a.m., just before the Tactical Patrol Force arrived, the ratio of protesters to cops was about seventy-five to one.

On Sunday, the next night, more than 100 cops faced a crowd much larger and more assertive than the first. Some people were chanting "Gay

ABOVE: **Gay rights demonstration at the Democratic National Convention, 1976.**
RIGHT: **Graffiti on a boarded-up Stonewall Inn window, 1969.**

> "If a bullet should enter my brain, let that bullet destroy every closet door in the country."
>
> —HARVEY MILK

power!" Others formed a kick line, singing, "We are the Stonewall girls / We wear our hair in curls / We don't wear underwear / We show our pubic hair." This was a reaction to a pattern of police harassment often experienced by transgender women at the bar.

Rain on the next two days dampened the protests. On Wednesday, the protesters returned for what was to be the final street battle, featuring threats of arson, looting, arrests, and injuries to participants on both sides. The riots were over, but a movement had begun.

In 1969, the Mattachine Society, one of the country's oldest gay rights groups, was eighteen years old. The Los Angeles founders were communists, but their influence diminished in the face of ongoing McCarthyism. However, until the mid-1960s, the society and its magazine both attracted supporters in the fight for gay rights and to some extent influenced public opinion.

By 1969, Mattachine had begun to move away from radicalism; its well-educated members, including many mature professional men, were put off by the rowdy, lawless aspects of the Stonewall riots. The original Christopher Street protesters represented a different segment of the gay community—the poorest, least respected one: drag queens, highly visible gay men and lesbians, homeless youth, and transgendered persons, who at the time found social acceptance in few other places.

Unsurprisingly, then, as the Mattachine Society grew more conservative and less willing to adopt confrontational tactics, it was less attractive to younger, more radical activists, and its influence declined.

Today, advocates for LGBT rights are not confined to those communities, and protections exist at the federal level as well as in many states and

municipalities. The ACLU files amicus briefs in rights cases, and Amnesty International has assisted some individuals to leave countries where their lives were endangered because of their sexual orientations.

Strong, successful LGBT organizations include the Human Rights Campaign, Lambda Legal, Gay & Lesbian Advocates and Defenders (GLAAD), the National Center for Transgender Equality, and the National Center for Lesbian Rights.

Since 1970, LGBT Pride (originally Gay Pride) month has been celebrated in June to commemorate the Stonewall riots. Greenwich Village preservationists secured the area near the bar in the National Register of Historic Places in 1999. On June 24, 2016, President Barack Obama dedicated the Stonewall National Monument. ■

LEFT: **National March on Washington for Lesbian and Gay Rights, 1979.**

AIDS CRISIS AND GAY RIGHTS MOVEMENTS OF THE '80s AND '90s

" "

I was known as the angriest man in the world, mainly because I discovered that anger got you further than being nice. And when we started to break through in the media, I was better TV than someone who was nice.

—LARRY KRAMER

TOP: **Larry Kramer posing in front of a bookshelf in his home, 1989.** LEFT: **Part of the AIDS quilt on display in Washington, DC, 2004.**

THE TUMULTUOUS DECADE of the 1970s, which saw the burgeoning of advocacy groups, including Lambda Legal and the National Center for Lesbian Rights, also saw the first Gay Pride month. It was a period of increased publicity about LGBT issues, social as well as legal, usually entailing discrimination based on sexual orientation and concomitant deprivation of rights. The energy of younger, more confrontational activists unleashed after the Stonewall riots of 1969 was often channeled into the disco scene, centered in clubs in the larger cities, and into the arts.

However, much of the optimism characterizing the '70s began to evaporate as a major health crisis gained steam. The first victims of the HIV/AIDS epidemic were identified in 1981 as gay men in Los Angeles. That same year, six gay men and some friends met in the New York City living room of writer Larry Kramer to discuss what was then called "GRID

(Gay-Related Immune Deficiency)" or "the gay cancer" to raise money for research. In 1982, the Gay Men's Health Crisis (GMHC) began to offer services for the prevention and cure of HIV/AIDS; its initial project was a telephone hotline. Also in 1982, four friends formed AIDS Project Los Angeles (APLA). This telephone hotline was located in the Los Angeles Gay and Lesbian Community Services Center, in a closet equipped with one phone.

Despite the efforts of GMHC, APLA (now APLAHealth), and other outreach groups to spread awareness in the gay community, the new plague did not seem to alarm the majority of gay men. They did take note on October 2, 1985, when actor Rock Hudson died in his sleep of AIDS-related complications. Although Hollywood friends had long known or suspected that Hudson was gay, it was newspaper and magazine articles that made his sexual orientation a matter of general knowledge.

The coverage accorded HIV/AIDS for the two years after Hudson's death helped activist organizations and fund-raisers, but the goodwill didn't last. The number of AIDS patients was outpacing the development of therapeutic regimens for the disease, and death tolls mounted. An atmosphere of discouragement among patients and their caregivers was complemented by a preference on the part of much of the public to hear fewer downer stories about gay men, often young, who were dying of an incurable disease. The intravenous drug users, hemophiliacs, and Haitians, who comprised nearly half the AIDS population, received even less attention in the media.

In 1986, the entire LGBT community received a drastic, unexpected blow. The Supreme Court upheld the constitutionality of a Georgia law that made criminals out of consenting adults who had oral and anal sex in private. The law applied to heterosexual as well as homosexual partners, but the defendant in *Bowers v. Hardwick* was a gay man.

The decade of the 1990s got off to a promising start with the founding of the National Lesbian and Gay Journalists Association, which has become a force in securing balanced press coverage of gays and lesbians. Many of these men and women now take their place among fellow professionals in the mainstream media; others bring their skills to specialized LGBT publications.

In general society, though, 1990–1999 was another decade marked by concern about AIDS, which in 1992, and again in 1994, was the leading cause of death for U.S. men between the ages of twenty-five and forty-four. Tony Kushner won the 1993 Pulitzer Prize for Drama for his stunning play about AIDS, *Angels in America*. Also that year, the film *Philadelphia* told the story of a gay lawyer, played by Tom Hanks, who loses his job when it's discovered that he has AIDS.

Progress in AIDS treatment came about in 1995 when the U.S. Food & Drug Administration approved the first protease inhibitor, a drug used in retroviral therapy. The picture brightened further in 1996, the first year since the epidemic began in which diagnosed cases of AIDS declined in the United States. In 1997, the U.S. Centers for Disease Control and Prevention announced the first substantial decline in AIDS deaths in the country.

Although *Bowers v. Hardwick* would not be overruled until 2003 (in *Lawrence v. Texas*), the Supreme Court in *Bragdon v. Abbott* declared people in the early stages of HIV disease to be eligible for the protections of the Americans with Disability Act, like people with the full-blown disease.

In addition to the almost annual milestones reached in the 1990s, gay social and political issues began to receive national attention. Legislation at the state and federal levels was matched by local initiatives introduced by advocates for LGBT rights and countered by conservative "pro-family" groups. Issues included controversies involving gays in the military, same-sex marriage, adoption, hate crimes, and discrimination against LGBT people in hiring and employment.

The period 1980–1999 was one of continuing struggle. But patience and the advances many had worked to bring about would pay off in the new millennium. ■

"WE WON'T DIE SECRET DEATHS ANYMORE. THE WORLD ONLY SPINS FORWARD. WE WILL BE CITIZENS. THE TIME HAS COME. BYE NOW. YOU ARE FABULOUS CREATURES, EACH AND EVERY ONE. AND I BLESS YOU: MORE LIFE. THE GREAT WORK BEGINS."

–TONY KUSHNER, *ANGELS IN AMERICA*

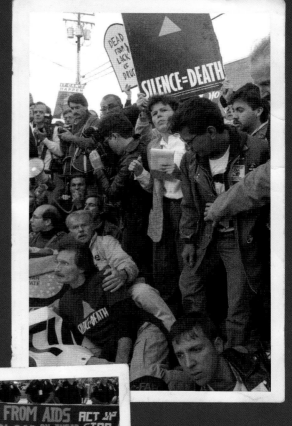

ABOVE: **Protesters hold up signs at an ACT UP protest in front of the FDA in Maryland, 1988.**
LEFT: **ACT UP members stage a protest in San Diego, CA, 1996.**

MARRIAGE
EQUALITY

" "

I believe one day a "ban on gay marriage" will sound totally ridiculous. In the meantime, I will continue to speak out for equality for all of us.

—ELLEN DEGENERES

TOP: **Justice Anthony Kennedy, 2011.**
BOTTOM: **Tammy Baldwin, the first openly gay member of the U.S. Senate, 2013.**
LEFT: **Supporters rejoice outside the Supreme Court after same-sex marriage is legalized across America, 2015.**

THE FIRST LEGALLY sanctioned same-sex marriage in the world united Helene Faasen and Anne-Marie Thus, of the Netherlands, in the year 2001. Also in that year, Arizona repealed its sodomy laws. Similar advances, including the passage of laws outlawing discrimination based on sexual orientation and gender identity in some U.S. states, occurred between 2002 and 2006 in Africa, Australasia, Canada, Central America, the Middle East, and South America as well as the United States and Europe. Julie Ann Peters's

Luna was the first young-adult novel from a mainstream U.S. publisher to have a transgender character. The first transgender person to win statewide office in Hawaii was Civil Rights Commissioner Kim Coco Iwamoto.

By 2006, opposition from anti-gay voters in nine U.S. states led to the banning of same-sex marriage and/or civil unions and to the voiding of antidiscrimination legislation. However, progress resumed in 2007 with more worldwide gains in civil union and partnership laws, a trend that has continued ever since. And although reservations about the acceptability of homosexuality continued strong in the three Abrahamic faiths, the Reconstructionist Rabbinical Assembly named a lesbian rabbi, Toba Spitzer, as its president in 2007, and Joy Ladin became the first openly transgender professor at an Orthodox Jewish institution, Stern College for Women of Yeshiva University.

In 2008, a man convicted of first-degree murder in the killing of Angie Zapata, a transgender woman from Greeley, Colorado, was the first person in the United States to also be convicted for commission of a hate crime against LGBT peoples. The story of the victim was featured on the television show *Aqui y Ahora* the next year.

Long-sought legal rights appeared worldwide in 2009, as the path to adoption by same-sex couples advanced in Finland (covering stepchildren only) and nonrelatives as well as step-children in Scotland. Meanwhile, same-sex marriage rights continued to be granted, one by one, by U.S. states. In 2009 and succeeding years, the total of LGBT persons in elected and appointed political positions continued to climb. In addition, pride parades and marches, which originated in the United States in 1970, were held for the first time in countries that limit their citizens' freedoms in many areas.

A long-awaited breakthrough occurred in 2011: the U.S. government's policy of barring from military service openly gay, lesbian, and bisexual people, as exemplified by Bill Clinton's "Don't Ask, Don't Tell" policy, came to an end. The policy also forbade harassment of or discrimination against service personnel or applicants and had other provisions that gave LGB individuals who wanted to remain in the service no choice but to stay in the closet. The machinery to rescind the policy, initiated during President Barack Obama's first term, took most of a year to run its course.

LGBT rights reached the United Nations in 2011 when the UN Human Rights Council approved a resolution, introduced by South Africa, requesting a study on discrimination and sexual orientation. The vote was close—twenty-three for, nineteen against, three abstentions—but the ice had been broken. The resolution, identified as A/HRC/17/L.9/Rev1, was the first document affirming LGBT rights to be approved by any UN body. Two years later, the UN held its first meeting on the rights of LGBT persons.

With *Obergefell v. Hodges*, the U.S. Supreme Court's landmark "gay marriage" decision, still three years away, a same-sex Israeli couple made history by seeking a divorce from the Ramat Gan Family Court; it was granted in 2012. In the same year, the first openly lesbian U.S. senator was elected (Tammy Baldwin of Wisconsin), as was the first openly bisexual member of Congress (Kyrsten Sinema of Arizona).

The military too advanced lesbian and gay service members. In 2012, Brenda Sue Fulton and Penelope Dara Gnesin were married in West Point's Cadet Chapel; it was the first non-heterosexual union to be solemnized there. Also in 2012, Army officer Tammy

Smith became the first openly gay active-duty general in American history; the ceremony took place at the Women's Memorial at Arlington National Cemetery. A year later, Autumn Sandeen was notified by the Navy that the Defense Enrollment Eligibility Reporting System had been updated to show her gender as female. This veteran, a transgender woman, seems to have been the first person whose gender change was officially recognized by the Department of Defense. In 2013, Kristin (formerly Chris) Beck, a retired Navy SEAL, published *Warrior Princess*, an account of her military career and her transition. She was the first member of that elite unit to announce such a change.

As the decade rolled on, LGBT rights received support from a little college town in the Deep South and from the queen of England. Starkville was the first city in Mississippi to pass an antidiscrimination resolution that included LGBT citizens. Elizabeth II, in praising a forty-year-old institution, the London Lesbian and Gay Switchboard, became the first British monarch to offer such a public affirmation.

Support for LGBT individuals reached to previously inhospitable places in 2014. Several thousand Cypriots watched the nation's first Gay Pride parade; seventeen-year-old Pascal Tessier, an openly gay Boy Scout, became an Eagle Scout; and in Turkey, tens of thousands of spectators turned out for the Istanbul Pride parade, the largest pride parade in a Muslim country. However, two years later, the parade, which had started in 2013 with thirty marchers, was banned by local authorities.

Barack Obama, who had clarified his stance on same-sex marriage repeatedly during his career as a politician, made an additional significant gesture on LGBT issues in 2015. In declaring May to be National Foster Care Month, he stated explicitly that sexual orientation or gender identity shouldn't prevent anyone from becoming an adoptive parent or a foster parent.

RIGHT: **President Obama addresses the Annual Human Rights National Campaign Dinner, 2009.**

The Fight for Gay Rights   119

The period following 2015, the year of the *Obergefell* decision, saw additional firsts for LGBT people, with greater recognition of transgender persons and their rights worldwide as well as decriminalization of homosexuality in tradition-bound, often isolated island groups the world over. The story continues to unfold.

The U.S. Supreme Court's opinion in *Obergefell* was delivered by Associate Justice Kennedy, who was joined by Associate Justices Ginsburg, Breyer, Sotomayor, and Kagan. Chief Justice Roberts filed a dissenting opinion in which he was joined by Associate Justices Scalia and Thomas, who also filed separate dissents and joined each other's, and by Associate Justice Alito, in which Scalia and Thomas joined.

In the four years that elapsed between the de facto repeal of the Defense of Marriage Act (DOMA) and the *Obergefell* decision, activists had worked steadily to build a legal foundation for just such a case. Lawsuits were pursued in the lower courts, popular referendums were held, and some state legislatures legalized same-sex marriage. Also importantly, public approval of same-sex marriage—which had exceeded 50 percent in 2010—by mid-June 2015 stood at nearly 60 percent.

During the same period, "Love Is Love" became a Facebook meme, and Obama inserted the phrase in his Rose Garden speech on the day of the Supreme Court's historic ruling. The Love Is Love movement comprises compassionate individuals who wish "to protect and promote the existence of love, for oneself and for others, no matter one's sexual orientation, gender, religion, race, or age." ∎

RIGHT: **Celebrations at a Gay Pride parade in France, 2014.**

"I'M NOT THE BIGGEST FAN OF THE WORD 'PARTNER.' IT EITHER MEANS THAT WE RUN A BUSINESS TOGETHER OR WE'RE COWBOYS. 'BOYFRIEND' SEEMS FLEETING, LIKE MAYBE WE MET TWO WEEKS AGO. I'VE BEEN SAYING 'BETTER HALF' FOR AS LONG AS I'VE BEEN ABLE TO. I THINK IT'S A LITTLE SELF-DEPRECATING AND CLEARLY DEFINES THAT WE'RE IN A RELATIONSHIP, BUT IT WOULD BE NICE TO SAY 'MY HUSBAND.'"
—NEIL PATRICK HARRIS

"

No union is more profound than marriage, for it embodies the highest ideals of love, fidelity, devotion, sacrifice, and family. In forming a marital union, two people become something greater than once they were. As some of the petitioners in these cases demonstrate, marriage embodies a love that may endure even past death. It would misunderstand these men and women to say they disrespect the idea of marriage. Their plea is that they do respect it, respect it so deeply that they seek to find its fulfillment for themselves. Their hope is not to be condemned to live in loneliness, excluded from one of civilization's oldest institutions. They ask for equal dignity in the eyes of the law. The Constitution grants them that right.

The judgment of the Court of Appeals for the Sixth Circuit is reversed.

It is so ordered.

—JUSTICE ANTHONY KENNEDY

ABOVE: The White House stands illuminated in rainbow
lights in support of gay marriage, 2015.

RESIST
ST
THE GONG S
RES
HAVE
SERVE
RESIST
ESIST
RESIST
RESIST
RESIS

TRANSGENDER
RIGHTS

❝ ❞

Our LGBTQ students...deserve to live their lives as themselves... And they deserve elected leaders who believe in them, who don't legislate against them, who insist on the words of St. Francis de Sales: "Be who you are and be that well."

—DANICA ROEM

DESPITE THE RESPECT and acclaim extended to many celebrity transgender persons—from Jan Morris to Laverne Cox—men and women in the process of transformation, those too young to have achieved professional attainments, and those in between often experience discrimination that has no broad-spectrum legal remedy. Only eighteen states have antidiscrimination laws that specifically protect transgender persons. Other states, following President Trump's 2017 revocation of his predecessor's guidance to public schools with respect to bathrooms, are seeing suits that would enact bathroom and other restrictions.

Transgender persons are disproportionately at risk from physical attacks by those who seem to oppose their very right to exist. Laws imposing penalties for hate crimes don't benefit any victims, whether traumatized, wounded in body, or dead. Therefore, some transgender activists are interested in partnering with Black Lives Matter and other minority groups that share their concerns about criminal justice reform and gun violence.

The 1990 Americans with Disabilities Act does not cover gender identity disorder, although LGBT advocates hope that transgender persons exhibiting gender dysphoria, a type of anxiety that can be treated medically, will qualify. The court case, *Blatt v. Cabela's Retail, Inc.*, seeking redress for outright discrimination against a transgender woman in Pennsylvania, ruled that individuals who suffer from gender dysphoria are protected by the ADA.

As anti-trans legislation in the U.S. military and school systems continues to be explored by the Trump administration, others, such as Danica Roem, push back. Roem, a journalist who was recently elected to the Virginia House of Delegates—edging out Republican candidate Bob Marshall, self-described as Virginia's "chief homophobe"—became the first openly transgender person to be elected in U.S. state legislature. As we look to the future, key wins such as Danica's will pave the way to true equality for the trans community. ■

LEFT: **San Francisco City Hall is lit pink and blue for Transgender Day of Remembrance, 2017.**
RIGHT: **Maria Keisling, executive director of the National Center for Transgender Equality, speaks during a press conference covering the transgendered servicemember ban, 2017.**

"I BEGAN TO BELIEVE
VOICES IN MY HEAD—
THAT I WAS A FREAK,
THAT I AM BROKEN, THAT
THERE IS SOMETHING
WRONG WITH ME, THAT I
WILL NEVER BE LOVABLE...
YEARS LATER, I FIND THE
COURAGE TO ADMIT
THAT I AM TRANSGENDER,
AND THIS DOESN'T MEAN
THAT I AM UNLOVABLE."
–LANA WACHOWSKI

HOW TO GET INVOLVED

IN THE FIGHT FOR GAY RIGHTS

RESEARCH • SPEAK OUT • VOLUNTEER
TALK • LISTEN • DONATE • MARCH • VOTE
CALL YOUR LOCAL REPRESENTATIVES
START YOUR OWN ORGANIZATION!

WHETHER INDIVIDUALS IDENTIFY as LGBT while in middle school or after years of closeted loneliness, they can find friendship, as well as moral and political support, in many organizations. Those who have experienced litigable physical harm or discrimination can readily find groups that offer legal support.

Perhaps the premier U.S. organization for LGBT rights is the Human Rights Campaign (HRC) (hrc.org). More than 1.5 million people belong to HRC or support it in its work to secure LGBT equality. Suggestions for involvement range from the physically active ("keep on marching" and signing up to volunteer) to actions that publicize the cause in a nonconfrontational way that signifies commitment. Examples in the second category include signing HRC's "No Hate in My State" pledge and displaying a sticker with the organization's logo, a bright yellow equal sign on a deep blue background; bumper stickers are also available.

Volunteering opportunities are listed on the websites of well-known rights advocates such as the American

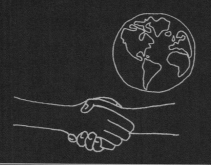

Civil Liberties Union (aclu.org/issues/lgbt-rights) and the Southern Poverty Law Center (splcenter.org). Volunteers are also needed on an ad hoc basis at election time and whenever a specific cause moves you to fight for it.

Important advances in LGBTQ equality have begun through legislation. Conversely, today lawmakers in your state or county may be considering discriminatory regulations. Learning what laws apply in your area can suggest names of legislators to contact with encouragement or short summaries of why you believe a given measure is good or hurtful. Supporting a candidate may mean going outside your own congressional district. Once signed up, you may receive assignments that can be completed from home, such as helping out in social media campaigns.

The U.S. office of Amnesty International, based in Washington, DC, provides opportunities for everyone to get involved—LGBT people, their families, friends, and loved ones, plus advocates for justice and equality who work to eradicate discrimination. Its website

(amnestyusa.org) has links for educational materials and for actions needing participants.

Ever since 1970, the year of the first Gay Pride parade in New York City, LGBT people and their supporters have been marching. Whether you travel to major events in a big city or participate in marches in your home area, these displays of pride and solidarity demonstrate the strength of demands for respect and equality. Marching isn't for everyone, but for young people, especially, it can be an exhilarating experience.

Those who prefer to do their volunteering indoors are always welcome to help with telephone hotlines, homeless shelters (which in many cities serve a substantial LGBT population), or office work in established centers. Attorneys, paralegals, and qualified counseling professionals are also in demand. If none of these suit, remember that two venerable organizations, the Gay Men's Health Crisis and APLA (now APLAHealth) began with small meetings of a few friends. ■

THE FIGHT FOR WORKERS' RIGHTS

1886

FOTLU dissolves itself and, with a different roster of member unions, is renamed the American Federation of Labor (AFL).

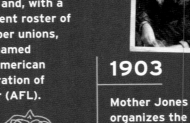

1903

Mother Jones organizes the March of the Mill Children from Philadelphia to New York.

1919

Samuel Gompers chairs delegation at the Versailles Peace Conference that creates the International Labor Organization (ILO).

1881

The Federation of Organized Trade Labor Unions (FOTLU) is founded in Pittsburgh, PA.

1882

The first Labor Day parade in the United States is held in New York City.

1899

The National Consumers League is formed to address child labor and other issues.

1913

The U.S. Department of Labor is established in a law signed by outgoing president William Howard Taft.

1913

President Woodrow Wilson appoints William B. Wilson as the first secretary of labor.

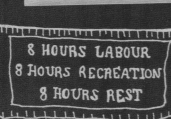

8 HOURS LABOUR
8 HOURS RECREATION
8 HOURS REST

1938

President Franklin D. Roosevelt signs the Fair Labor Standards Act, establishing the first national minimum wage and mandating the forty-hour week.

1947

Over presidential veto, Congress passes the Taft-Hartley Act, which has substantial negative impact on unions.

1964

The Civil Rights Act of 1964 is passed.

1980

Politician and activist Lech Walesa forms the Solidarity labor union.

2009

President Barack Obama signs the Lilly Ledbetter Fair Pay Act, named after the 1979 plaintiff.

Equal Pay

1935

In *Schechter v. United States*, the Supreme Court declares the National Recovery Act of 1933 unconstitutional.

1946

The number of strikers in the United States passes over 4 million.

1963

President John F. Kennedy signs into law the Equal Pay Act of 1963.

1963

Hundreds of thousands participate in the March on Washington for Jobs and Freedom.

1965

The Voting Rights Act of 1965 is passed.

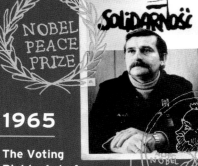

SOLIDARNOŚĆ

NOBEL PEACE PRIZE

2016

The Equal Pay Act is amended again, prohibiting wage discrimination between men and women doing the same work.

1983

Lech Walesa is awarded the Nobel Peace Prize.

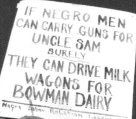

IF NEGRO MEN CAN CARRY GUNS FOR UNCLE SAM SURELY THEY CAN DRIVE MILK WAGONS FOR BOWMAN DAIRY

Negro Labor Relations League

NATIONAL HEADQUARTERS

MARCH ON WASHINGTON FOR JOBS & FREEDOM

WED. AUG. 28

LABOR PROTESTS
IN EARLY U.S. HISTORY

" "

Society is always taken by surprise at any new example
of common sense and of simple justice.

—RALPH WALDO EMERSON

TOP: **Samuel Gompers, 1901.**
LEFT: **Colored engraving of police officers dispersing the striking employees of Streetcar in New York, 1886.**

STRIKES BY ORGANIZED workers have been around since workers began to organize more than 3,000 years ago. The first such labor action seems to have been mounted by artisans in ancient Egypt, who laid down their tools to protest nonpayment of wages in the reign of Pharaoh Ramses III. History tells us royal officials rectified the matter.

While not organized workers in the modern sense of the term, the skilled Egyptians were united at a single time and place by trade, by employer, and by grievance. A millennium would pass before artisans and merchants began, separately, to form associations in towns and cities. The guilds also were not workers' organizations in today's usage, since the members themselves controlled the prices—the demand for skilled workmanship exceeded the supply in many places.

Colonial America followed the medieval labor hierarchy of master craftsmen above journeymen, who in turn had risen from apprentice status. However, in the difficult pre-Revolutionary economy, New York business owners were feeling the pinch. Thus in 1768, when one merchant had announced that journeyman tailors' wages, already low, would be reduced, the tailors agreed amongst themselves not to work at all at the new rate. They knew that because men with their skills couldn't be quickly replaced, the merchant stood to lose profits if he had no clothes to sell. The merchant saw things the same way and did not reduce the tailors' wages. This work stoppage in the colonies seems to have been unprecedented, and historians tend to regard it as a one-time event.

Eleven years after the end of the Revolutionary War, the economy was expanding, and entrepreneurial master cordwainers (shoemakers) saw an opportunity to try a new business model. They would produce cheaper shoes at lower cost to be offered to new customers near and far. One way to lower production costs was to reduce the wages of the producers, journeyman cordwainers. To protect their traditional wages, in 1794

journeymen in Philadelphia formed the first sustaining workers' organization: the Federal Society of Journeymen Cordwainers.

Over the next few years, members called several "turn-outs" aimed at preventing other shoemakers from accepting wages lower than the standard wages. These actions were aimed less at employers than at strikebreakers—"scabs," according to one of today's definitions of the term. By 1805, the Cordwainers had established a strike fund, the first of its kind. Setting up such reserves has been standard practice, where possible, ever since. Management is often motivated to settle a dispute in the favor of workers if a hefty union strike fund would support nonworking members in an action lasting more than a few days.

In the pre-industrial era, many of the grievances that later riled working men, women, and children were virtually nonexistent and could be dealt with on a case-by-case basis. Higher pay was often an issue, but the workers had acquired skills during their

apprenticeships and from years on the job; often they worked from home or on premises dedicated to their art or craft.

Today's U.S. labor movement took shape gradually in the nineteenth century, taking its impetus from a five-year economic depression in the 1870s and from the efforts of such foresighted leaders as Samuel Gompers. During this period, the unions served skilled workers in the building trades and other traditional occupations.

Urgent matters of overlong hours, unsafe working conditions, and child labor would come to the fore in the next generation, when grueling, low-paying factory work was all that was available to many men, women, and children, native born and, increasingly, immigrants. ■

> "WE CANNOT SEEK ACHIEVEMENT FOR OURSELVES AND FORGET ABOUT PROGRESS AND PROSPERITY FOR OUR COMMUNITY... OUR AMBITIONS MUST BE BROAD ENOUGH TO INCLUDE THE ASPIRATIONS AND NEEDS OF OTHERS, FOR THEIR SAKES AND FOR OUR OWN."
>
> —CESAR CHAVEZ

FIRST LABOR DAY PARADE

THE COUNTRY'S FIRST Labor Day parade was held in New York City on September 5, 1882. Led by a brass band, 400 union men set off from City Hall Park in Lower Manhattan, heading north on Broadway. They were greeted by jeers at first, for many Americans scorned workers in general, especially trade unionists. However, as additional contingents of marchers joined the parade on the way to 42nd Street, the crowd grew and became enthusiastic. After the obligatory speeches, 10,000 marchers and thousands of onlookers crowded onto the El, New York's elevated train system, for the after-party. Picnic fare, music, and games were provided by the event's organizers, the New York Central Labor Union, in Wendel's Elm Park, a green space west of Central Park. ∎

FEDERATION OF ORGANIZED TRADES AND LABOR UNIONS

" "

Look at the killing of the men in the mines, in the mills, in the factories, and in the shops. Oh! it is an awful price we pay for our prosperity and our progress. Higher price than is paid in any country on the face of the globe.

—SAMUEL GOMPERS

TOP: **Samuel Gompers at the Republican National Convention in Chicago, 1908.**
BOTTOM: **Robert M. Ammon, leader of the Pittsburgh and Fort Wayne railroad strikes, 1877.**
LEFT: **Illustration of Lebanon Valley Railroad bridge burning by Pennsylvanian railroad strikers, 1877.**

THE PARENT ORGANIZATION of the American Federation of Labor, which in 1955 became the American Federation of Labor and Congress of Industrial Organizations (AFL-CIO), had the ungainly name of Federation of Organized Trades and Labor Unions (FOTLU). FOTLU was a result of a worldwide economic recession that struck in the United States on September 18, 1873. A major Philadelphia bank failed on that day, followed immediately by other trusted financial institutions. In the accompanying panic, the New York Stock Exchange closed for ten days, playing havoc with the manufacturing, construction, and railroad industries.

Between 1873 and 1879, some 18,000 U.S. businesses declared bankruptcy. Unemployment was high, as jobs disappeared all over the country; craftsmen, as well as men who did physical labor, found themselves out of work. Many who remained employed suffered huge wage cuts. Strikes by railroad workers often turned violent, eliciting harsh responses from company police as well as local law enforcement agencies. A forty-five-day strike by railroad workers in 1877 was brought to an end by local and state militias and federal troops; railroad workers then began to organize into unions.

By 1873, a national union of cigar makers was already nine years old. Future labor leader Samuel Gompers, who had begun to learn the craft as a child in England, was a stalwart of a local cigar makers' union in New York City. He developed the position that an organized trade union movement offered working people a surer route to economic progress than the political activism advocated by the Marxists and socialists who were influential in the international labor movement.

Gompers favored a "new unionism," focusing not on political goals but on the issues working people faced every day. His industry, cigar making, was changing for the worse as entrepreneurs imposed the assembly-line workplace on artisans who had traditionally worked in their homes or in small shops. The cigar makers made very little money; many lived and worked in tenement houses

under deplorable conditions. Gompers called in the city board of health to force the tenement owners to make improvements. His success persuaded the Brotherhood of Carpenters and Joiners and other unions to adopt new unionism's principles.

In November 1881, Gompers represented the Cigar Makers' International Union at a national convention in Pittsburgh attended by delegates from 110 labor organizations, including the powerful Knights of Labor (KOL). After much discussion, the delegates voted to form FOTLU; its resolutions called for support of the eight-hour day, limitations on child labor, and other progressive goals.

FOTLU was to be short-lived. Disagreements arose between the Knights of Labor and the craft unions, concerned that the KOL, then growing more radical, would provoke crackdowns on all organized workers. In December 1886, after months of negotiations, FOTLU voted to dissolve itself, turning its assets and property

over to the other delegates, who included a number of craft unionists from the KOL. The men renamed their organization the American Federation of Labor. ■

ABOVE: From *Harper's Weekly*, illustration titled "The Great Strike" of the Sixth Maryland Regiment fighting its way through Baltimore rioters, 1877.

KNIGHTS OF LABOR

" "

The only effective answer to organized greed is organized labor.

—THOMAS DONAHUE

TOP: **American Women's Trade Union League at the 1886 convention of the Knights of Labor.**
BOTTOM: **Print of the leaders of the Knights of Labor, with Terence V. Powderly in the center of the wreath, 1886.**

THE KNIGHTS OF Labor (KOL) were a powerful force in the labor movement of the 1870s and 1880s. Like other unionists, they fought for higher pay and better working conditions for their members; they wanted to make the eight-hour workday the national standard. Other long-term goals were more progressive: abolition, not regulation, of child labor; and equal pay for equal work. The KOL admitted women and African Americans to their ranks before the other labor federations did. With some exceptions, their policy was to avoid strikes.

That changed in 1885 when railroad baron Jay Gould, who controlled the Wabash line in the Southwest, laid off KOL shopmen, prompting union members employed on other railways to refuse to operate any train that had Wabash cars in it. The unexpectedly large display of union solidarity led Gould to negotiate with union president Terence Powderly, who called off the strike. The parties agreed that there'd be no surprise walkouts as long as management kept the door open to discussions. Within months, KOL membership rose sevenfold, exceeding 700,000 in mid-1886.

The labor peace was not to last. On March 1, 1886, another Gould railroad, Texas & Pacific, fired a foreman in Marshall, TX, for attending a union meeting on company time. Irate, other workers uncoupled cars and took over switch junctures. Gould responded by hiring scabs to restore service and Pinkerton detectives to back them up. He also requested help from the states affected, for soon more than 200,000 workers were striking in Arkansas, Illinois, Kansas, Missouri, and Texas. The Great Southwest Railroad Strike was under way.

As the situation deteriorated, it seemed that although Powderly had failed to control his workers, Gould was bent on destroying the whole union. Violence continued, but management stood firm, oblivious to union demands; a congressional committee investigated, negotiations failed, violence from both sides escalated, and the public turned against the strikers. The strike was called off on May 4.

The Knights of Labor, battered by membership losses and adverse public opinion, some of it stemming from fake news, did not continue after 1886, but many of its members joined the new American Federation of Labor. ∎

RIGHT: **Illustration of the arrest of a striker during the Texas railroad strike in 1886.**

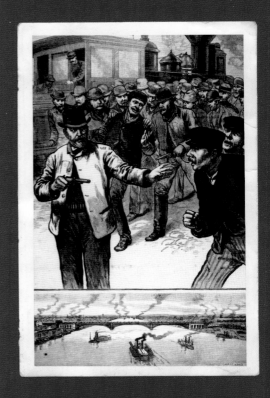

"THE MOST HEROIC WORD IN ALL LANGUAGES IS REVOLUTION."
—EUGENE V. DEBS

BREAD AND ROSES **STRIKE**

" "

It is absolutely foolish to say the strike "happened without any apparent cause," "that it was lightning out of a clear sky," etc. As a matter of fact, it was a harvest, it was a result of seeds sown before.

—JAMES P. THOMPSON

TOP: **William B. Wilson, the first U.S. Secretary of Labor, 1913.**
BOTTOM: **The Everett Mill in Lawrence, MA, 1933.**

THE NINE-WEEK-LONG BREAD and Roses strike began on January 11, 1912, at the Everett Mill in Lawrence, Massachusetts, when weavers, mainly immigrant women, stopped work and the noisy mills went silent. A representative of management who went to the plant floor to investigate was told: "Not enough pay." The English was entirely clear.

The mill official realized what was happening. A recent state law had cut the work week for women and children by two hours, down to fifty-four hours, and the workers had just learned that employers had cut their wages proportionately. The average weekly wage, now averaging $8.44, would have meant skipped meals for most.

The next day workers at other mills walked off the job and into the ice and snow, with the backing of their union, the Industrial Workers of the World (a.k.a. the Wobblies). IWW men with knives stormed the Everett Mill, disabling machinery and ruining work materials. The police beat them with clubs. By the end of the next day, the number of strikers exceeded 10,000.

Marchers sang and chanted as they demonstrated in the snow-packed streets. State militiamen with bayonets protected the plants, and women joined the men, picketing, marching, and speaking out at rallies. The women's banners expressed twin demands, a living wage and dignity: "We want bread and roses too."

As word of the strike spread, workers elsewhere in Massachusetts and beyond came through with collections, while local farmers donated food. Wobblies organizers on the scene coordinated these efforts, but no one had expected the polyglot, multiethnic textile workers to demonstrate such solidarity of purpose. Meanwhile, the mill owners and municipal authorities hired troublemakers to discredit the strikers, and on January 29, a mob attacked a streetcar carrying workers from a rival union, the United Textile Workers. Two young protesters were killed, one by police and the other by a militiaman's bayonet; martial law was declared.

On February 10, with no end in sight, strikers' families started shipping their young sons and daughters out of the state. Many had relatives in Manhattan, and sympathizers who knew none of the strikers also volunteered to feed and shelter the children. The first train, bearing 119 children, was greeted by 5,000 cheering New Yorkers at Grand Central Station. The children who arrived the next week marched down Fifth Avenue. These publicity coups, arranged by the IWW, were a boon for the strikers but not for their opposition in Lawrence. Accordingly, police were waiting on February 24 when a third wave of children arrived at the Lawrence train station. Despite the city marshal's orders to disperse, mothers tried to help their children board.

What happened next raised a national outcry: police dragged the women away by the hair, beat them with clubs, and arrested them. There were many injuries and one miscarriage. President Howard Taft called for an investigation, and on March 2 Congress began a hearing. Workers, including children who'd dropped out of school before age fourteen, testified to the brutal conditions in the mills. Adults spoke of low pay and the diminution of buying power due to the wage reduction.

Health and safety were other important concerns. A mill worker's life expectancy was less than forty years. Physicians testified to the prevalence of slow deaths from chronic respiratory infections and tuberculosis exacerbated or brought on by inhalation of dust and lint. Horrendous workplace accidents took lives and limbs, leaving many mutilated. Legislators and the public alike were shocked by the experience of fourteen-year-old Carmela Teoli, whose scalp had been torn off by a mill machine.

The immense public sympathy for the strikers that had been generated by the children's witness persuaded the mill owners that it was time to rethink their initial response to the demand for more pay. The agreement proposed included a 15 percent raise in base wages, a smaller hike in overtime pay, and a promise of no retaliation against the strikers.

The Bread and Roses Strike ended on March 14 at a meeting on Lawrence Common. Fifteen hundred workers voiced agreement to accept the employers' offer; there were only five dissents. By the end of the month, 275,000 more New England textile workers received raises, and other industries took up the trend.

Almost a year later, on March 4, 1913, his last day in office, President Taft signed a law establishing a new cabinet-level department, the Department of Labor, to "foster, promote, and develop the welfare of the wage earners of the United States, to improve their working conditions, and to advance their opportunities for profitable employment."

The first labor secretary, William B. Wilson, was appointed the next day by the new president, Woodrow Wilson. Secretary Wilson, a Scottish-born labor leader, former international officer of the United Mine Workers of America, and chair of the House Committee on Labor from 1911 to 1913, served in the cabinet until 1921. ■

RIGHT: **The children of striking workers in Lawrence, MA, are provided with food at the Labor Temple in New York while their parents hold the line, 1912.**

TOP: **100,000 shopmen walk out at the Northwestern Railway Yards in Chicago, 1922.**
BOTTOM: **Workers on strike stand by covered trucks on a Seattle street, 1919.**
LEFT: **State troops march through Boston during their tour of duty following the strike of policemen.**

REPRESSION AND DEPRESSION

STRIKE WAVE

" "

Labor cannot stand still. It must not retreat. It must go on or go under.

—HARRY BRIDGES

BARELY THREE MONTHS after the Armistice of 1918, Seattle shipyard workers struck, protesting government wage controls that had been in place for two years. However, federal regulators rejected the request of 35,000 union members for a postwar pay hike. In response, on February 6, 1919, the Metal Trades Council (MTC) called a strike, closing down the yards. The MTC, a union coalition, appealed to the city's Central Labor Council, whereupon most of Seattle's 110 local unions voted for a sympathy walkout.

The 25,000 participants included the American Federation of Labor (AFL) and Industrial Workers of the World (IWW) members.

The Central Labor Council declared an end to the country's first citywide general strike on February 11. Consistent with the general climate of anti-unionism that prevailed at the time, police and anti-union goons had been harassing and arresting left-wing activists. Radicalism in the Pacific Northwest had been strong since the 1917 revolution in Russia, and Seattle

> "In our society it is murder, psychologically, to deprive a man of a job or an income. You are in substance saying to that man that he has no right to exist. You are in a real way depriving him of life, liberty, and the pursuit of happiness, denying in his case the very creed of his society."
>
> —DR. MARTIN LUTHER KING JR.

businessmen feared that U.S. workers might revolt as well. Catching the implications of this attitude, many union members began returning to their jobs days before the strike ended.

The Seattle walkout, although it fizzled, has historical importance as the country's first citywide general strike. In the fall of 1919, a larger labor action was to gain national attention. The grievance this time wasn't pay, it was about the freedom of Americans to organize themselves into unions. The issue came into focus on September 7, when the famed American radical Mother Jones was arrested for trying to hold a union meeting in tiny Duquesne, Pennsylvania, home to a U.S. steel mill. Unrest in the coal and steel sector of western Pennsylvania was mirrored across the country throughout the summer of 1919, and a national committee of AFL

representatives from twenty-four union bodies set a strike date for September 22.

The strike's initial success was spectacular: four million workers, one in every five industrial workers in America, walked off the job; almost half the country's steel industry was shut down. Surprised and alarmed, the steel industry moved to turn public opinion against the strikers. This wasn't hard, given fears that had surfaced earlier in Seattle. During this new "red scare," state police in Pennsylvania beat picketers with clubs and jailed thousands of protesters on any charges they could devise; sometimes immigrant status sufficed. In October, martial law was declared in Gary, Indiana, another steel town, where unionists had been attacked by strikebreakers and police.

Infighting between AFL leadership and the powerful iron-, steel-, and

tinworkers union, some of whose members broke the strike by returning to work, hastened the strike's collapse on January 8, 1920. But it was nine months before the mills gave in and allowed workers to return to their jobs, sealing the union rout.

On the heels of the Seattle strike came another big-city labor action. The three-day Boston Police Strike was disastrous for the strikers, who were replaced, not rehired. Boston's police officers, chafing at long hours, pay that had remained the same for sixty years, and wretched conditions in the station houses, had begun expressing those grievances in 1917. When they voted to join the AFL and, on September 9, 1919, struck, the reaction was highly negative. Government and much of the public, already concerned about the spread of Bolshevism, had been

further spooked by a third strike in one year. At the urging of AFL head Samuel Gompers, the police ended the strike on September 12.

It was two years before another nationwide strike occurred, and this one too would collapse, but not before 400,000 strikers had called attention to another injustice in the compensation of employees of big corporations. The goal of the Railway Shopmen's strike of 1922 was to reverse a federally mandated cut in the hourly pay of maintenance and repair workers. The amount, seven cents an hour, was no small matter to workers at the low end of the economy in a period of inflation. The strike lasted two months: from July 1 to September 1.

The shopmen's strike featured a flaw in the union solidarity that had marked earlier actions. In 1922, members of the nine railroad unions not affected by the pay cut not only failed to join the shopmen's action but became strikebreakers, thus keeping the railroads going. Some strikers harassed and physically attacked the strikebreakers, while railroad company guards and local police shot strikers and uninvolved persons alike. Strikers also sabotaged trains and vandalized railroad property. The supporters of the strikers, often women, remained loyal, but as the public relations damage grew, the cause seemed to be lost.

Attempts to end the strike in July had failed, and soon Attorney General Harry Daugherty, comparing the strikers to Bolshevik leader V. I. Lenin, sent in U.S. Marshals. Eventually, President Warren G. Harding was persuaded that a negotiated settlement was appropriate and authoritarian violence was not. The outcome, far from a win for labor, came on September 1 in the form of an order from a federal judge: an injunction against union activities that included striking, assembling, and picketing. ■

UNITED AUTOMOBILE WORKERS
AND THE BROTHERHOOD OF SLEEPING CAR PORTERS

" "

I believe you should tell the story of injustices, of inequalities, of bad conditions, so that the people as a whole in this country really face the problems that people who are pushed to the point of striking know all about, but others know practically nothing about.

—ELEANOR ROOSEVELT

THE FLINT SIT-DOWN Strike of the United Automobile Workers against General Motors (GM) began on December 30, 1936, when the firing of two assembly line workers at the Cleveland Fisher body plant triggered a strike there. The union, which had been planning a strike at GM's Flint plant, called its workers in Michigan to action on the same day.

The sit-down strike proved to be a powerful tool for labor: if workers were barricaded inside a workplace, their employer couldn't carry on by hiring replacement workers. Moreover, if the workers had prepared for the strike and weren't destroying company property, eviction by force of arms wasn't an option. The workers at Flint had made detailed plans covering meals, exercise programs, and entertainment as well as a system of maintaining order among restless workers.

However, until 1936, management still held the upper hand. The United Automobile Workers (UAW), not yet two years old, was weak and knew it. Thus delegates who attended the first union convention in 1936 had decided to gain leverage by striking GM, the most powerful of the Big Three automakers.

The Flint action expanded to other GM plants, with violence on both sides, alarming the auto companies, the civil authorities, and the general public. Requested to send in the National Guard, Michigan governor Frank Murphy

first wavered, then refused. On the next day, February 11, 1937, GM officials signed a contract with the union that gained the members a 5 percent pay raise and relaxation of such workplace regulations as "no talking during lunch."

The agreement was GM's acknowledgment of the UAW as the sole bargaining representative between the company and union members. The arrangement was set to expire in six months, but the UAW had soon signed up 100,000 additional GM employees. The autoworkers' strike was the first major action of its parent union, the newly formed Congress of Industrial Organizations (CIO).

The year 1937 also brought an advance in the fight against racism in America. During the Reconstruction period, George Pullman had hired many former slaves to work on his railroad cars, always for long hours at low pay. He continued to exploit his employees into the boom years of the 1920s,

but railroad workers, who rationally feared being fired and knew they wouldn't be welcome in the AFL of the time, were reluctant to organize. They asked and received assistance and leadership from civil rights activist A. Philip Randolph, editor of the *Messenger*, a literary and political magazine by and for African Americans.

The Brotherhood of Sleeping Car Porters and Maids (BSCP) ("and Maids" was later dropped) was formed on August 25, 1925. The early years were hard, especially during the Great Depression, but persistence of BSCP leadership and a more favorable political climate thanks to the New Deal brought success: in 1935, the Pullman Company recognized the union, and the BSCP became the first labor union led by African Americans to receive an AFL charter. In 1937, the BSCP won its first contract. ■

LEFT, TOP: **Wives and mothers of the GM sit-down strikers show their support outside the plant, 1937.**
LEFT, BOTTOM: **Crowd of union members demonstrating against orders for the eviction of the sit-down strikers, 1936.**

FORTY-HOUR WEEK
AND THE CONGRESS OF INDUSTRIAL ORGANIZATIONS

" "

There is nothing laudable in work for work's sake.

—JOHN STUART MILL

TOP: **Female Woolworth's employees declare they are striking for a forty-hour work week, 1937.**
BOTTOM: **Parisian protesters crowd outside of the city hall for increased salaries and a forty-hour work week, 1937.**

THE GREAT DEPRESSION that followed the stock market crash of 1929 was a time of setbacks in the struggle for workers' rights, as survival took precedence over workplace grievances. Hundreds of thousands crowded into pop-up slums created all over the country by homeless, jobless people and their families, the collateral damage of the catastrophe.

Yet economic conditions remained bad for much of President Franklin D. Roosevelt's administration, which began in 1933. Businesses continued to suffer, and owners tried to keep costs down;

many insisted on long work days, kept wages low, and employed children in factories for as little as $4 a week.

The courts of the 1930s tended to support employers' right to conduct business as permitted by applicable state laws or in accord with broad constitutional principles. Workers' rights were another form of collateral damage. That damage was nowhere clearer than in the 1935 Supreme Court case of *Schechter Poultry Corp. v. United States*. The so-called sick-chicken case incorporated charges relating to two uninspected chickens sold by Schechter Poultry.

In *Schechter*, the Court unanimously declared the entire National Industrial Recovery Act of 1933 unconstitutional on grounds of unwarranted presidential delegation of powers and improper use of the congressional power to regulate interstate commerce. The NIRA protections that disappeared with the decision included maximum work hours allowed and unions' right to organize.

It took President Franklin D. Roosevelt five years to rectify the situation. Even buoyed by a landslide victory in the general election of 1936, he lost two rounds of voting on a bill to be called the Fair Labor Standards Act. Two years later, when congressional election results showed intense popular support, legislators began to bend. On June 25, 1938, Roosevelt signed the FLSA, which mandated a minimum wage and the forty-hour work week.

Another labor landmark in 1938 was the formation of the Congress of Industrial Organizations in Pittsburgh, in November. The AFL, founded back in 1886, consisted of craft unions, whose members were skilled in various trades, such as cigar making, the skill longtime AFL chief Samuel Gompers had honed since childhood. In the early twentieth century, noncraft American workers began to organize, and their unions—the miners, the steelworkers, the garment workers—joined the AFL.

John L. Lewis, the charismatic leader of the United Mine Workers (UMW) and at one time a top Gompers aide, secured the AFL's endorsement of "industrial unionism." In this organizational method, all the workers in a given industry belong to the same union, the semiskilled along with the skilled. The accompanying increase in union membership can be advantageous in dealing with large companies and conglomerates.

Lewis then formed, within the AFL, the Committee for Industrial Organization, which the parent union expelled in November 1938. That same month, Lewis saw to the conversion of the AFL committee into an independent organization, the Congress of Industrial Organizations, of which he was the first president. He headed the UMW for forty-one years, retiring in 1960. ∎

"BY EXTENDING THE WORKING DAY, THEREFORE, CAPITALIST PRODUCTION...NOT ONLY PRODUCES A DETERIORATION OF HUMAN LABOR POWER BY ROBBING IT OF ITS NORMAL MORAL AND PHYSICAL CONDITIONS OF DEVELOPMENT AND ACTIVITY, BUT ALSO PRODUCES THE PREMATURE EXHAUSTION AND DEATHOF THIS LABOR POWER ITSELF."

—KARL MARX

TOP: **An African American man in Chicago, IL, demonstrating against unfair labor practices, 1941.**

ECONOMIC AND SOCIAL JUSTICE

" "

In recognizing the humanity of our fellow beings, we pay ourselves the highest tribute.

—THURGOOD MARSHALL

THE GREAT DEPRESSION had caused immense suffering, but as the United States and other developed countries emerged from the decade that began with the market crash of 1929, hope emerged too. One expression of hope, which also contains a look backward, was Woody Guthrie's "This Land Is Your Land." Everyone knows the part about the redwood forest and the Gulf Stream waters. Less familiar is the verse in which Guthrie recalls the Depression. He recalls seeing "my people," waiting, hungry, by the relief office, and

wondering "Is this land made for you and me?" The 1940 song famously ends with a ringing affirmative.

Between 1940 and 1946, membership in the NAACP, which had been around since 1909, grew from 50,000 to 450,000. That period also saw gains in rights for African Americans. In 1941, with Europe at war, President Franklin D. Roosevelt wanted to be prepared, and he wanted any wartime effort that might be necessary to offer jobs to all citizens. Accordingly, in June 1941, he issued Executive Order 8802, which banned discrimination in the national defense industry and among subcontractors.

Defense jobs represented an important employment opportunity for black Americans, and civil rights activists had at first been concerned that black workers wouldn't be hired. Thus A. Philip Randolph, Bayard Rustin, A. G. Muste, and other leaders had been planning a march to protest racial discrimination in hiring for defense jobs. Upon learning of the executive order, Randolph called off the march, an immediate payoff in goodwill for the government.

In 1942, FDR reinstated a World War I institution, the National War Labor Board, and specified that there be union members. This move was enthusiastically received by the Congress of Institutional Organizations, which two years later—as Roosevelt prepared to run for a fourth term— went political. The labor organization set up the country's first political action committee to get out the union vote for the president. ■

STRIKE WAVE
OF 1946

" "

And remember: conformity means death. Only protest gives a hope of life.

—BERTRAND RUSSELL

TOP: **May Day workers parade in New York, 1946.**
BOTTOM: **Protesters demonstrating against President Harry S. Truman's threat to draft striking workers into the armed forces, 1946.**
LEFT: **Labor protesters hold signs demanding economic unity across races, 1930.**

THE GREAT STRIKE Wave of 1946 represented labor's pent-up grievances, unaddressed on the national level during World War II because many unions had taken a no-strike pledge to show their commitment to the war effort. Overwhelmingly, the issues were work rules, not pay. Forerunners to the wave began in 1945, just weeks after Japan's surrender: nearly 400,000 members of five unions struck in September, followed in November by a quarter-million autoworkers.

In January 1946, 174,000 electrical workers, 300,000 meatpackers, and 750,000 steelworkers struck. Unlike 1919, when authorities had brutally harassed striking steelworkers, the 1946 action was peaceful. It ended when, under pressure from President Harry S. Truman, the steel companies folded.

In April 1946, United Mine Workers president John L. Lewis called 350,000 coal miners to join an existing action. Railroad workers struck in May. With national stability threatened, Truman issued an ultimatum, which the union ignored. The president then went before Congress, seeking powers he knew the unions wouldn't want to face. While he was speaking, he was told that the strike had been settled, on his terms. The coal miners settled within days.

After a few months of peace, West Coast longshoremen struck in September, and union members at Firestone and Goodyear went on sympathy strikes to support steelworkers in southern Canada. Again a few months passed with no major work stoppages.

In December, an overreaction by the city council of Oakland touched off an unexpected chain reaction. Dozens of picketers, female clerks employed by two downtown department stores, were set upon by 200 police from Oakland and nearby Berkeley. Pushing people aside, the officers cleared the area and set up machine guns across from one store. Truck drivers and streetcar operators parked their vehicles where they stood, and everyone, passengers included, left the area.

Downtown workers arrived on the scene and decided to cooperate with the strikers. They cordoned off the central city, permitting anyone to leave but no one lacking a union card to enter.

Then union members marched to city hall to demand that the mayor and city council resign. When the Sailor's Union at Oakland's army base walked out, more than half the city's population of 200,000 was on strike. Walkouts spread to five neighboring cities.

In the end, AFL negotiators, overlooking the department store women's issues, secured the city council's promise not to use scabs again and ended the strike. The sellout was blamed on an Oakland Teamsters local, all of whose incumbent officers were voted out of office. The AFL ran candidates in the next city council election and took 80 percent of the open seats.

In the 1946 elections, anti-union sentiment dating back a half-century produced a return of control of the House to Republicans. Passage of the Taft-Hartley Act followed in 1947: Congress overrode a presidential veto on June 23. Taft-Hartley's provisions include a ban on jurisdictional strikes, closed shops, and union donations of money to federal political campaigns. The act, with amendments, remains in effect. ■

"THE LABOR MOVEMENT DID NOT DIMINISH THE STRENGTH OF THE NATION BUT ENLARGED IT. BY RAISING THE LIVING STANDARDS OF MILLIONS, LABOR MIRACULOUSLY CREATED A MARKET FOR INDUSTRY AND LIFTED THE WHOLE NATION TO UNDREAMED LEVELS OF PRODUCTION. THOSE WHO ATTACK LABOR FORGET THESE SIMPLE TRUTHS, BUT HISTORY REMEMBERS THEM."

—DR. MARTIN LUTHER KING JR.

MARCH ON WASHINGTON AND THE EQUAL PAY ACT OF 1963

" "

In this world, laws are written for the lofty aim of "the common good" and then acted out in life on the basis of the common greed... It is a world not of angels but of angles, where men speak of moral principles but act on power principles.

—SAUL ALINSKY

TOP: **Bayard Rustin, deputy director of the March on Washington, and Cleveland Robinson, chairman of the administrative committee, meet prior to the march, 1963.**

THE 1963 MARCH on Washington for Jobs and Freedom, 100 years after the proclamation of the emancipation of the country's slaves, was a protest against the ongoing deprivation of fundamental rights and privileges among the great majority of African Americans.

Leaders of established civil rights groups like CORE, NAACP, SCLC, and the Urban League formed an umbrella organization, the Council for United Civil Rights Leadership. Cochairmen were chosen: A. Philip Randolph, who had guided the creation of the Brotherhood of Sleeping Car Porters, and a deputy, Bayard Rustin, longtime civil rights volunteer and talented organizer.

The march organizers hoped for help from union leaders. UAW president Walter Reuther signed on and participated in the march. AFL-CIO head

George Meany declined to offer support. Some black activists hesitated, fearing that any instances of violence would discourage President John F. Kennedy from continuing to push for the civil rights legislation he'd promised in a speech on June 11.

As plans for the march firmed up, goals were announced. These went beyond jobs to include a nationwide minimum wage ($2/hour), the immediate end of segregation in the public schools, and strong measures to invoke constitutional protections against discrimination-based violation of civil rights.

The plans came to fruition on August 28, 1963, when a quarter-million people marched into history. Most (around 80 percent) were black, but tens of thousands of white supporters showed up as well. Rustin's logistics, which included the presence of 4,000 volunteer marshals in addition to the assembling and coordinating of marching divisions from all over the country, succeeded brilliantly. Dr. Martin Luther King's Jr.'s "I Have a Dream" speech

at the Lincoln Memorial evoked tears and cheers, as did the songs of Odetta, Mahalia Jackson, Bob Dylan, and others. Joan Baez led the crowd in "We Shall Overcome." Among the speakers were Randolph, Reuther, Rustin, the NAACP's Roy Wilkins, future congressman John Lewis, and Christian and Jewish clergy.

Five days later, Dr. King and others who'd spoken at the rally met with Kennedy at the White House. The president received them warmly, saying he believed the huge, well-managed protest had strengthened the chances of his civil rights bill. The Civil Rights Act did, of course, pass the next year, and President Lyndon B. Johnson carried on his predecessor's legacy by encouraging the passage of the Voting Rights Act of 1965.

The cause of eliminating what is now called gender discrimination in pay had a setback in the Supreme Court in 1979, which was rectified in 2009 by the Lilly Ledbetter Fair Pay Act, named after the plaintiff in the 1979 case. The Equal Pay Act was amended again in 2016; full equality remains to be achieved. ∎

INTERNATIONAL LABOR
ORGANIZATION

" "

Throughout history, it has been the inaction of those who could have acted, the indifference of those who should have known better, the silence of the voice of justice when it mattered most, that has made it possible for evil to triumph.

—HAILE SELASSIE

TOP: **Delegates gather at the 1919 peace conference in Versailles.**
LEFT, TOP: **A view of the crowd gathered at the March on Washington for Jobs and Freedom.**
LEFT, BOTTOM: **Demonstrators holding signs during the March on Washington.**

THE ARMISTICE OF November 11, 1918, put an end to World War I, which left 10 million dead and 20 million wounded. Before the peace negotiators convened in France, labor organizations in the United States and Europe, wanting a seat at the table, were recommending ways of protecting working people and their unions in the postwar world. The vehicle for addressing their concerns, created in 1919, was called the International Labor Organization (ILO). Originally part of the League of Nations, the ILO was folded into the United Nations when the UN replaced the League after World War II.

The AFL's Samuel Gompers chaired the Commission on International Labor Legislation at the Versailles Peace Conference in February 1919. The delegates agreed on the need to give the workers, employees, and government of each member nation a voice in discussions of political and economic matters. The ILO has worked for nearly a century to advance longstanding labor demands with respect to hours of work, wages, and workplace safety. ILO conventions on minimum wages have been produced and updated since 1928. Today the organization has 187 state members. North Korea doesn't belong; other nonmembers are smaller states like Monaco.

Child labor remains an issue in some countries, and the existence of forced labor in the twenty-first century has prompted ILO programs to raise awareness of these abuse as well as human trafficking. The organization works with governments affected to come up with laws, action plans, and training materials. The branch called ILOAIDS, established in 2010, not only assists with research, technical support, and policy as AIDS affects the workplace, but also protects the rights of HIV-positive workers.

An original goal of the ILO, to secure a lasting global peace, has proved elusive, but in the twenty-first century, in developed countries, labor disputes usually are settled bloodlessly. Employers would rather negotiate than cope with negative publicity. Similarly, strikers provoked to the point of violence can throw rocks or engage one-on-one with police, but seriously damaging today's well-protected means of production is seldom an option. ■

LEFT: **The International Labor Conference in Geneva, 1929.**
RIGHT: **Photograph from the peace conference held in Versailles, France.**

TOP: **Lech Walesa, founder of Solidarnosc Trade Union, 1981.**
BOTTOM: **Gdansk shipyard workers on strike await negotiations between Walesa and Polish leader General Jaruzelski, 1980.**

LECH WALESA AND THE SOLIDARITY MOVEMENT

" "

Every moment is an organizing opportunity, every person a potential activist, every minute a chance to change the world.

—DOLORES HUERTA

THE RISE AND triumph of Solidarity in Poland provides a case study. "Solidarnosc," the short form of "Independent Self-Governing Labor Union," refers also to a social movement in Poland that brought together workers like marine electrician Lech Walesa, one of its founders, and also the Catholic Church and representatives of the anti-Soviet left, who were mainly intellectuals. The first local chapter was formed with government permission at Walesa's workplace, the Lenin Shipyards in Gdansk, on August 31, 1980. In September, a national organization came to be: NSZZ ("Underground Solidarity") consisted of other free trade unions committed to the struggle to achieve social change and advance workers' rights in Poland.

From the outset, Solidarity had open support from the AFL-CIO and covert support from the CIA. However, like the rest of Poland the organization faced a serious obstacle when General Wojciech Jaruzelski imposed martial law on December 13, 1981. In addition to being a military officer, Jaruzelski was the highest ranking Communist Party official in Poland. Although it was clear that martial law was intended to crush the union, repressive and threatening measures affected all Poles: the six-day work week, more censorship, tanks in the streets. Strikes and demonstrations were followed by arrests; thousands were detained.

Walesa, who had been arrested in December 1981, was released in November 1982, but not before Jaruzelski outlawed Solidarity. In the weeks that followed, four demonstrators were killed and more than 10,000 activists were arrested. But Radio Solidarity was already in operation, and within months NSZZ would have more than 70,000 members.

International opinion was also behind Solidarity: President Ronald Reagan, Labour and Conservative British leaders Margaret Thatcher and Tony Benn, national officers of European Communist parties Santiago Carillo of Spain and Enrico Berlinguer of Italy, and the Polish-born pope, John Paul II, revered as an advocate of social justice, peace, and freedom, all supported the cause. A face-saving way out was needed, and Jaruzelski found one: on July 22, 1983, the period of martial law was declared over. Barely three months later, Walesa was awarded the Nobel Peace Prize, which his wife accepted in Oslo because the Polish government refused to give the laureate a passport.

Economic conditions continued to worsen, not only in Poland but throughout the Eastern bloc, including the USSR. In 1985, a new Soviet leader, Mikhail Gorbachev, the first president of the USSR, was forced to initiate reforms, setting in motion a trend that was mirrored the next year in Poland. There, political prisoners were released, amnesty was declared, and on September 30, 1986, Walesa and others established the first legal entity since 1981 to include the Solidarity name.

However, the national economy was on its last legs and in 1989 Jaruzelski legalized the original Solidarity and agreed to hold elections. The vote, which has been described as "partially free," gave Solidarity candidates ninety-nine out of one hundred Senate seats and made Jaruzelski president by one vote. Despite the overwhelming rejection of the Communist Party, Jaruzelski tried, but failed, to co-opt Walesa. Another presidential election was held in 1990, and Walesa was the winner.

As president of Poland, Lech Walesa instituted some controversial reforms, but his efforts to initiate a market economy bore fruit, and the country grew rapidly. Although issues of style and temperament led to his defeat for reelection in 1995, and to a subsequent defeat in 2000, Walesa has received many honors and has had the satisfaction of seeing Poland become a full member of NATO (2000) and a member of the European Union (2004). ∎

CHILD LABOR **LAWS**

" "

Someday the workers will take possession of your city hall, and when we do, no child will be sacrificed on the altar of profit!

—MARY HARRIS "MOTHER" JONES

TOP: **Mother Jones and her army of striking workers start out for a march to New York, 1903.**
BOTTOM: **Grace Abbott, Chief of the Children's Bureau of the Department of Labor, 1929.**

THROUGHOUT HISTORY, CHILDREN have worked long and hard, often without pay, in family enterprises such as farming or small businesses. Later, job opportunities opened up for small, controllable people who could be compelled to do simple, repetitive tasks for very low wages. These were the factory jobs that budding industrialists offered to the poor as a means of monetizing, however slightly, the children parents couldn't afford to feed.

Two primary components of the Industrial Revolution, which began in Britain in the mid-eighteenth century, were technological advances and cheap labor. That poor people flocked to accept factory work at low wages is unsurprising. The simultaneous rise in the number of working children wasn't immediately apparent.

Little kids had been doing farm work for centuries, helping parents who were serfs in feudal Europe or doing chores on farms in colonial America. No doubt there were abuses, but normally parents assigned age-appropriate jobs to their children. Six-year-olds could gather eggs, for example; they weren't expected to put in a full day.

Then came the Industrial Revolution, and with it new problems and new job descriptions. Facilitating shop floor maintenance by scurrying around and under heavy equipment could be accomplished by children after minimal instruction. Production could be increased by downsizing individual workspaces. Workers who could squeeze into small spaces were also useful in U.S. and European mines.

Child labor, and the abuses that inevitably accompanied it, developed unimpeded for several generations. However, in 1832, an American trade group, the New England Association of Farmers, Mechanics, and Other Workingmen issued a condemnation of child labor. Four years later, the country's first child labor law was passed and participants at the National Trades' Union Convention proposed state minimum-wage laws for factory work. These measures alone would prove insufficient.

Opposition to child labor emerged in Europe at the same time. The British passed the Factory Act in 1833 and the Mines Act in 1842. Both laws limited the ages at which children could be employed; the Factory Act established minimum work hours for children aged nine to thirteen.

In continental Europe, Karl Marx, who had been speaking out against child labor since the 1840s, later not only condemned the practice of using child workers but emphasized the consequences of depriving children of education. In the States, the AFL began agitating for state laws banning wage labor for children in the early 1880s.

Early in the twentieth century, the exploitation of child labor and the abuse of the child workforce became an issue. In 1903, Mother Jones, a fierce opponent of child labor, organized the March of the Mill Children, a three-week hike by child and adult textile workers from Philadelphia to New York in support of an ongoing strike. In 1904 an advocacy group was formed in New York City, the National Child Labor Committee. The U.S. federal government and some states tried to regulate the conditions under which children were employed; those opposed pursued their cases up to the Supreme Court. The Court's decisions turned on the justices' interpretation of states' rights, as guaranteed by the Tenth Amendment and on the Constitution's Commerce and Contract Clauses; children's welfare was dismissed as tangential.

Not all parties to Supreme Court cases took the children's side. *Hammer v. Dagenhart* (1918) originated with a suit by a man whose children had been put out of work by a federal law banning from interstate commerce goods produced by child labor. The father won. In *Bailey v. Drexel Furniture* (1922), an IRS official sought enforcement of a law that imposed a 10 percent tax on profits of mines and quarries that employed children younger than sixteen. The government lost.

Yet even as children were being killed and maimed in workplace accidents, succumbing to lung and respiratory ailments, and missing out on education that might have opened up a path out of poverty, people were speaking out. One such advocate was Grace Abbott, a social worker who was director of the U.S. Department of Labor's Children's Bureau from 1921 to 1934. She wrote this often quoted statement:

Child labor and poverty are inevitably bound together, and if you continue to use the labor of children as the treatment for the social disease of poverty, you will have both poverty and child labor to the end of time.

Grace Abbott had retired from the Children's Bureau, and the Great Depression was well under way in 1938 when Congress passed the Fair Labor Standards Act. This law set a national minimum wage that mandated overtime pay, established standards for recordkeeping, and regulated the employment of children under the ages of sixteen (agricultural work) and eighteen. Amendments have strengthened this protection.

The "youth employment" portion of the FSLA was a product of decades of work by nongovernmental agencies

Children participate in an anti-child-labor demonstration at the 1909 Labor Day parade in New York.

including the National Child Labor Committee, founded in 1904; the National Consumers League; and individual activists like Mother Jones, who had begun her career as a labor organizer when she was a widow with young children.

Today, child labor law violations in legal enterprises in the United States are virtually nonexistent. Elsewhere in the world, flagrant abuses of working children are gaining increased attention, especially when the products made are sold in developed countries at prices FSLA-compliant firms can't match.

Child labor, often forced, is found today in undeveloped countries and isolated regions worldwide. The U.S. Department of Labor tracks abuses by country and by category of goods. Children work in enterprises that are dangerous (mining, fireworks), degrading (pornography), and physically exhausting (making bricks and garments, stoop labor). Child tobacco workers absorb unhealthy amounts of nicotine through the skin; child miners, as well as agricultural workers and leather workers, are exposed to toxic chemicals.

Despite advances in the twenty-first century, in 2013 the International Labor Organization reported totals of 168 million child laborers, 85 million of them doing hazardous work.

Labor law has always been about leveling the working field—when it comes to wages, hours, and working conditions, employers almost always have a considerable edge over employees. This is especially true today, since large corporations and franchise operations account for many jobs. Moreover, union membership has been dropping all over the world since about 1970, with U.S. union membership down to 11.3 percent of the working population in 2013.

The Great Recession of 2009 seems to have canceled out union membership gains made in the 1980s. However, other causes have been cited. These include increased reliance by employers on temporary, part-time, and foreign workers, as well as the growth of the low-paid, hard-to-organize service sector.

It's also true that a strain of animosity to organized labor has existed since the earliest days, when violent, disruptive strikes and overblown "red scares" turned much public opinion against U.S. unions. But violence by police, corporate thugs, and state militias led many white-collar and nonunionized workers to support organized labor. And favorable strike settlements that resulted in higher pay and other benefits attracted new members or encouraged people to start their own unions. Public support for unions has decreased but almost always polls above 50 percent.

Looming in the background of labor gains and losses and shifts in public opinion is a 1947 law, passed over President Harry S. Truman's veto: the Labor-Management Relations, or Taft-Hartley, Act. The law made organizing more difficult and outlawed mass picketing, sit-down strikes, and other practices that labor had found helpful. With the backup of Taft-Hartley, a decades-long period of what has been called union busting began in the 1970s

and continues. Many believe that over time, the repressive employer strategies enabled by the 1947 law have helped depress union membership.

An aspect of Taft-Hartley that has assisted employers wishing to keep unions from their workplaces is the law's ban on card check, or majority sign-up. Card check was a tool used to great effect by the AFL and, later, the AFL-CIO, notably in the hands of United Mine Workers president John L. Lewis. It worked like this: Employees of a union who were seeking to organize were asked to sign cards assenting to the move in a setting that allowed the union reps and fellow workers, some of whom were union sympathizers, to know how everyone voted. As soon as a majority had signed cards, the union received automatic recognition. If such recognition wasn't achieved on the first ballot, holdouts were sometimes threatened with bodily harm or otherwise intimidated.

A law intended to restore card check to legality, the Employee Free Choice Act (EFCA), was introduced in Congress in 2005 but didn't become law then, nor when reintroduced in 2007. It also failed in 2009 despite support from Barack Obama, first as senator and then as president. In September 2012, Coca-Cola workers in Texas voted by secret ballot against being represented by the Teamsters. As of 2018, chances that the 115th Congress will pass the EFCA are slim. ■

HOW TO GET INVOLVED

IN THE FIGHT FOR WORKERS' RIGHTS

RESEARCH • SPEAK OUT • VOLUNTEER
TALK • LISTEN • DONATE • MARCH • VOTE
CALL YOUR LOCAL REPRESENTATIVES
START YOUR OWN ORGANIZATION!

YOU CAN TAKE action to support workers' rights and organized labor without belonging to a union. Some of labor's strongest supporters have jobs in fields that have never been organized (for example, most white-collar work); others work in industries that have consistently resisted unionization for their lower-level employees (bank tellers are a prime example).

As usual, volunteering at the local level is likely to be the most productive path, at least to begin. Starting can be as simple as looking around you for unorganized workers or union locals who need help. Agricultural areas will have one set of problems; Rust Belt locations that have lost many jobs will have another. However, often underlying infrastructural givens work against the prospects of major advancements in the near future.

In that case, you can be guided by your interests or by what's available in your area. Start by visiting websites of unions you admire even if they have no locals near you. Although the electricians, the longshoremen, and the Teamsters don't post volunteer opportunities, at

teamster.org/campaigns you can find an array of issues in play all over the country. The United Automobile Workers website (uaw.org/take action) has specific lobbying suggestions, which can be considered if participation is out of the question.

You can lobby those who make policy and law at all levels by phone, letter, or email. Studies have found that online petitions have little influence on those targeted. Adding one more canned message to a busy person's inbox is similarly ineffective, except perhaps near an election if the busy person's seat is imperiled. Phone calls can help, and some members of Congress and local officials are surprisingly accessible. There's one way to find out.

In lobbying for union rights, going negative can sometimes be more effective than a push for benefits that have little chance of being granted at present. If "Fight for $15" is a nonstarter in your area, you can work against candidates, nominees, or local referendum issues that seem to promise unfavorable consequences. On the other hand, if peaceful minimum-wage protests are sympathetically received, you'll be welcome to join in, with or without a sign.

Another source of ideas is Working America, a community affiliate of the AFL-CIO founded in 2003. This organization of more than 3 million nonunion advocates for good jobs and a fair economy has an impressive record of electoral victories. The website (workingamerica.org) suggests joining the group and following it on Facebook and Twitter, among other things.

The Los Angeles Alliance for a New Economy (laane.org) is a national grassroots group founded in 1993. Its members, many of them service workers, immigrants, or both, team up and go door to door, encouraging people to register to vote and to support labor issues. When targeting individual injustices, the group often favors civil disobedience. The leaders have identified populations needing help. Some affect working people in the areas of mortgage financing and student loan debt. A union-specific cause is the organization of bank tellers. ■

THE FIGHT FOR MODERN CAUSES

1997

The UNFCCC parties adopt the Kyoto Protocol in Kyoto, Japan.

2001

In the wake of 9/11, the Patriot Act gives the U.S. government new powers to investigate individuals suspected of being a threat, raising fears for civil liberties.

1976

The United Nation's International Covenant on Civil and Political Rights goes into force.

1976

The U.S. Supreme Court, in *Estelle v. Gamble*, rules that failure of a Texas prison to provide appropriate care to a prisoner injured on a work detail constituted "cruel and unusual punishment."

1994

The Death with Dignity Act is established in Oregon, legalizing physician-assisted suicide.

1999

The Columbine High School massacre occurs in Littleton, Colorado, the perpetrators killing thirteen people and injuring twenty-one others.

2001

U.S. Congress passes the No Child Left Behind Act. The act was controversial, as it withheld funding for schools that scored poorly on assessment tests.

2005

The U.S. Supreme Court upholds the Death with Dignity Act in *Gonzales v. Oregon*.

EDUCATION FOR BLACK AND BROWN YOUTH!

OCCUPY YOUR MIND

BAILOUT THE PEOPLE NOT THE BANKS

2011

The first day of Occupy Wall Street kicks off on September 17, protesters camp at Zuccotti Park in Lower Manhattan. The last of the protesters are cleared from the park on November 15.

2013

Edward Snowden leaks reports from the NSA's global surveillance program, including an order that showed they had obtained phone data from over 120 million Verizon users.

2015

The UNFCCC parties adopt the Paris Climate Agreement by consensus.

2016

California becomes the fifth state to allow physician-assisted suicide with the California End of Life Option Act.

2016

The U.S. Sentencing Commission reports a 49.3 percent national recidivism rate.

2018

Study is released that shows billionaires made enough money in 2017 to end extreme poverty seven times over.

2012

Sandy Hook Elementary School experiences a horrific school shooting, resulting in twenty-seven deaths.

2012

WikiLeaks reveals a U.S. Department of Homeland Security report that calls for surveillance of Occupy Wall Street protesters.

I AM MORE THAN A TEST SCORE

2015

By 2015, the United States has 5 percent of the world's population and 20 percent of the world's prisoners (2.5 million).

2015

No Child Left Behind is replaced by the Every Student Succeeds Act.

2017

On Earth Day, the March for Science takes place in Washington, DC, and in hundreds of cities across the world, advocating for evidence-based science and quality science education.

2017

President Donald Trump announces the United States' withdrawal from the Paris Climate Agreement.

2018

A nineteen-year-old former student opens fire at Marjory Stoneman Douglas High School in Parkland, Florida. Survivors of the shooting lead nationwide protests against NRA funding and gun violence.

PROTECT CHILDREN NOT GUNS!

TOP: **Doctor Andrew Wakefield awaits the General Medical Council's verdict on his unethical vaccine research case, 2007.**
BOTTOM: **Supporters of Wakefield gather outside the General Medical Council, 2007.**
LEFT: **Bill Nye joins protesters on Earth Day in Washington, DC, for the March for Science Rally, 2017.**

CENSORSHIP
OF SCIENCE

" "

The ability of scientists to present their findings to the scientific community, policy makers, the media, and the public without censorship, intimidation, or political interference is imperative.

—THE AMERICAN METEOROLOGICAL SOCIETY

A LARGELY INEFFECTIVE attempt to censor science arose when American parents bought into a theory, since thoroughly debunked, that childhood vaccines containing thiomersal cause autism and other health problems. In 1998, Briton Andrew Wakefield was one of the authors of a paper, published in a respected medical journal, that suggested a link between autism, irritable bowel disease (IBD), and routine vaccinations. The idea spread quickly among parents of autistic children seeking a reason for the condition.

Soon other parents were deciding to "protect" their offspring from the fearsome developmental disorder by depriving them of vaccination.

Careful reading of the paper would have shown that a study evaluating only twelve children, one-third of whom *didn't* develop symptoms of autism or IBD, was far from dispositive. However, many parents clung with a religious fervor to the belief that the vaccine was bad. Not much later, negative information about unethical, unprofessional behavior by Wakefield began to appear, and in 2010 he was banned from ever again practicing medicine in Britain.

But most anti-vaxxers remained convinced that the mercury-based preservative thimerosal had sickened their children and threatened any who might receive it. Moreover, the opponents' numbers grew as parents all over the country refused to allow their children the protection youngsters had long benefited from. The number of unvaccinated elementary school children increased, childhood diseases not seen in decades began to surface, and anti-vaxxers continued to find support. Politician Robert F. Kennedy Jr., who published a book on the subject, was joined by dozens of B-list celebrities.

Concern that the tide might be turning in the anti-vaxxers' favor lurched upward in early 2017 when Donald Trump, both as president-elect and as president, said he was considering a special autism commission. Kennedy has repeatedly stated that if such a commission is formed, he will head it.

For years, the media has been debunking the anti-vaxxer myths, in lead articles in national newspapers and news magazines, in medical journals, and in well-regarded websites like WebMD. Educational materials geared to people at all levels of schooling are readily available. Paradoxically, some of the most passionate anti-vaxxers are upper-middle-class parents with college degrees.

It is hard to explain this willful ignorance and the durability of this popular attempt to censor the use of science in debunking a fallacious idea with serious public health consequences. Yale Law School professor Dan Kahan suggests a cognitive approach to such conundrums of inflexible resistance to facts and overwhelming scientific consensus. Kahan is best known for his attempts to explain why climate-change deniers reject or dispute the veracity of "the science" with respect to climate change today and the magnitude of the threats the phenomenon represents. He's found that the more deniers learn about climate research, the more firmly they

adhere to their original beliefs, which tend to be supported by their cultural associations and values. The same may be true of the anti-vaxxers.

By the same token, the characteristics of the relatively small anti-vaxxer community can be observed among the larger population of those who reject scientific findings related to climate change. Obviously the voluminous data sets used in the study of climatology can be plugged into different models, which have led to different, sometimes opposing, interpretations. In climatology, the 1998 "hockey stick" graph, showing the dramatic increase in global warming since the Industrial Revolution, has its determined critics.

Nor is it surprising that opponents of the existing consensus among 97 percent of climatologists fall back on arguments used against science from the time of Galileo, who publicly supported a theory that's been paradigmatic for centuries now, not to mention concerted industry-funded campaigns to sow uncertainty. Today, the supporters of a defrocked physician, whose harmful late-twentieth-century suggestion took on a life of its own among well-meaning people, continue to attack conclusive contradictory evidence. Similarly, though with far less impressive backing, the opponents of the climate-change consensus maintain their circumscribed views. ■

WEALTH AND
OCCUPY WALL STREET

" "

This movement...is expressing dissent to the system itself...
It's saying that we believe the system itself is radically
corrupted, and we no longer are willing to tolerate it.

—GLENN GREENWALD

MOST PEOPLE ARE aware that wealth, or net worth, isn't the same as income, or the inflow of economically valuable items, such as cash. Growth in wealth among low-wealth people isn't necessarily achieved by an increase in income; decreases in wealth among the very rich may not follow even substantial drops in income. The more important variable in assessing the place of wealth in any society is distribution: gross imbalances in wealth distribution often give rise to income inequality issues.

All over the world, regardless of the degree of national economic development, wealth is more inequitably distributed than income. For any number of reasons, some people in every country are better off than others, but the amount that separates the very rich from the middle class in developed countries has become noticeably high. The wealth gap between the very rich and the working poor in the United States is much larger than that between the very rich and the middle class; the jobless poor are off the low end of the charts.

However, statistics can be

misleading, and comparing raw figures showing who has the most and the least wealth with those showing who receives the most and the least income is like comparing apples and oranges. To get an objective but imperfect sense of income inequality, it's helpful to start with the Gini index. This century-old measurement tool uses available national statistics to produce a single number representing the distribution of income among a country's residents. National statistics will always vary in quality and in factors measured, but comparison of two sets of numbers for the same country is a good place to begin.

Ratings according to the Gini index run between 0 (representing a country in which everyone has the same income, regardless of source) and 1 (a country in which all the income is distributed to one person and everyone else receives nothing). Simply put, the higher the Gini index, the greater the inequality; the lower the Gini, the more nearly equivalent the population studied.

However, every country has income disparities, which makes it interesting to compare the difference between the ratio of the Gini index for the richest 10 percent to the poorest 10 percent (call it ratio A) with the ratio for the richest 20 percent to the poorest 20 percent (call it ratio B). A 10 percent figure that is much higher than the 20 percent figure is an indication of income disparity that may lead to social unrest. A glance at a table of such data from 2010 reveals patterns suggesting that income inequality may stem from reasons other than unbridled greed, income similarity may reflect either good planning or nationwide hard times, and the benevolence of the government in place can influence the level of popular satisfaction.

For example, a slight difference between ratios A and B may characterize a small, stable country with a long-established social welfare system: Denmark, the Netherlands, Sweden, Norway, and the United Kingdom have differences between 2.2 (Norway and Sweden) and 6.7 (Netherlands). Also posting small differences are very poor countries struggling with the aftermath of civil wars (Bosnia-Herzegovina, 1.6),

invasion (Cambodia, 4.9), and natural disaster (Ethiopia, 2.3). The United States is an outlier: with a difference between ratios A and B of 6.5, this large country offers many benefits in the form of transfer payments, yet lacks a single-payer system of health insurance, and in 2016 had 45 million people under the poverty line, as well as 536 billionaires—the most in the world.

A considerably larger difference between ratios A and B suggests additional problems: ongoing civil wars (Central African Republic, at 36.5, is dead last in the UN's Human Development Index), or a coup d'état, natural disaster, or epidemic lawlessness (Honduras, 42.2). In the case of an unusually large disparity (Namibia, 50.5), the profits available from the country's gold, silver, diamond, uranium, and base metal mines suggest a society in which heavy income streams flowing to some citizens are not being shared.

Given the diversity of national situations and results, there's no worldwide answer to the problems caused by wealth inequality. However,

ABOVE: Occupy Seattle protesters stand off with officers during a May Day rally and anti-capitalist march in Seattle, Washington, 2012.

in the United States in 2011, the mainly young activists of Occupy Wall Street (OWS) thought they knew what was responsible: "the monied corruption of [American] democracy" was how Micah White, PhD, a cofounder of the OWS movement, put it in a reflective article on the *Guardian*'s website in 2017.

September 17, 2011, was day one of the two-month occupation of Zuccotti Park, renamed Liberty Square— "America's own Tahrir," in the words of early promotional material. The protest began with a rally and march to the park, where a temporary city was set up according to plan. The original complement of occupiers was estimated at around 100; over time, overnighters numbered between 30 and 200. Daytime visitors, including the media, were often much more numerous.

The organizers intended the park campsite to be a living symbol of the #OWS movement, and sympathizers soon appeared, spreading from the metro New York area to cities across the country, where peaceful marchers by the scores, hundreds, and thousands chanted "We are the 99 percent!" and "This is what democracy looks like!" Large unions also pitched in, with physical and financial support of a movement protesting social and income inequality as well as corporate greed and corruption.

The Zuccotti Park scene, with its enthusiasm and discord, comforts and inconveniences, celebrities and homeless comrades, received much coverage throughout its short lifetime. In the end, sanitation concerns forced the issue: on November 15, armed with authorization from the park's corporate owner, police began to clear the park. Some protesters left voluntarily; there were around 200 arrests.

Subsequent attempts to reoccupy the park, on New Year's Eve 2011, and on three occasions in 2012, were short-lived, with total arrests exceeding 300. Activists then focused on occupying banks, corporate headquarters, board meetings, college campuses, and foreclosed homes. Another recent initiative, Strike Debt, used donated funds to buy some students loans, which it then forgave. ■

"THE ISSUE OF WEALTH AND INCOME INEQUALITY IS THE GREAT MORAL ISSUE OF OUR TIME, IT IS THE GREAT ECONOMIC ISSUE OF OUR TIME, AND IT IS THE GREAT POLITICAL ISSUE OF OUR TIME."
—BERNIE SANDERS

FREE SPEECH

" "

Silencing a bigot accomplishes nothing except turning them into a martyr for the principle of free expression. The better approach, and the one more consistent with our constitutional tradition, is to respond to ideas we hate with the ideals we cherish.

—AMERICAN CIVIL LIBERTIES UNION

TOP: **Pro-LGBT protester in Italy waves an image of Putin wearing makeup. The image, which went viral in 2013, is banned in Russia and is considered "extremist material," and Russians who share the image on social media can face fines or even imprisonment.**
BOTTOM: **Portrait of John Milton, author of *Areopagitica*, circa 1629.**

AS ISSUES GO, "free speech" is a relative newcomer. The printing press had been around for 200 years before John Milton published his *Areopagitica* to protest the chilling effect of censorship by England's parliament in 1644. By the eighteenth century, the Enlightenment philosophers, well along in the development of their novel ideas about human freedom, had come to understand that the concept would be unworkable without freedom of expression, in speech and in the press. They were moved to this realization by the obstacles to the exchange of information due to the strict censorship then imposed by parliaments and by religious organizations.

Strict governmental censorship is present today only in highly authoritarian states. In Central America, the Middle East, Africa, and throughout Asia, violations are egregious and the punishments of those accused of illegal speech are extreme. The prisons of Cuba and Syria hold untold numbers of political prisoners—critics of the regimes who are silenced and tortured for expressing their opinions; some are executed, others die of starvation, illness, or injuries.

Detainees may be held in isolation for months or years without trial, on charges neither they nor their families ever learn. Those released often retain scars resulting from torture; in Aleppo, Syria, many of the thousands released in 2014 after the yearlong siege of Central Prison had tuberculosis as well. Those who walk free in Cuba after years of imprisonment aren't released en masse. Rather, international pressure, often including the plea of a highly respected person, such as Pope John Paul II or Gabriel Garcia Marquez, has preceded the release of a fortunate few.

Reports from China, Eritrea, North Korea, and Uzbekistan are infrequent to nonexistent because of the degree of government control over media. Those governments' unabashed, frequently successful attempts to prevent the free expression of ideas continue; criticism is ignored or blown off as interference with national sovereignty.

In the West, speech has never been freer, as profanities and obscenities of all kinds are accepted in public utterances, in popular songs, and in broadcast and print media, with the occasional bleep or "F——it!" Ironically, it often seems that the only effective brake on free speech is self-censorship. Yet it works, whether it's a five-year-old saying, "Oh, sh... sugar!" in front of parents or a public figure referring to "the other party" or "our friends abroad," knowing full well that the audience would prefer a more colorful description.

However, the civility option, essentially a call for self-restraint, is hard to promote in times of great passion. The difficulty is even greater because of the availability of so many platforms from which to express and amplify opinion. The proliferation of social media has encouraged many to "speak out" in highly provocative ways, whether in performance art uploaded to YouTube, in inflammatory rants posted on Facebook and in popular blogs, or in tweets. Excess encourages retweets and reposts; thoughtful commentaries on complex issues are relegated to print media, often magazines or Sunday reviews.

For good or for ill, the present atmosphere of almost total permissivity is closer to "free-range speech" than to the Enlightenment model of free speech, often encapsulated in terms of Citizen A's willingness to defend to the death the right of Citizen B to say things A finds distasteful.

U.S. Supreme Court cases over the past forty years have trended toward protection of forms of speech that had long been considered distasteful. In *Texas v. Johnson* (1989), the Court declared unconstitutional laws in effect in forty-eight states that banned the disrespectful burning of the American flag. It was a step beyond *FCC v. Pacifica Foundation* (1978), which ruled that while comedian George Carlin's "Filthy Words" routine was indecent, the government agency could determine the contexts in which "indecent" materials might be broadcast. Conversely, the "Bong Hits 4 Jesus" case (*Morse v. Frederick*, 2007) affirmed the authority of schools to suppress student speech under certain circumstances.

Clearly, freedom of speech in the United States now includes freedom to speak, write, or otherwise disseminate statements some will find distasteful or offensive. Two questions arise immediately: What, if anything, can be done to halt the deliberate publication of statements known to be false by their maker, often speaking anonymously? And how can a civil society be achieved when the public is constantly exposed to more or less plausible statements that may not be true?

Because the answer to the first question is obviously "nothing," finding a good answer to the second is critical. One response relies on a distributed approach to information vetting. That is, people with knowledge about the matters covered by a given statement take the time to do the necessary vetting and publish the results in an appropriate forum. A former secretary of state will write a letter to the editor of the *New York Times*; a hardcore Kardashian fan, who may have as

much cred with the celebrity culture as the one-time cabinet officer has with *Times* readers, will take to Twitter or Facebook. Other knowledgeable commenters will follow, and the erroneous statement will be discredited.

The secretary and the Kardashians are extreme examples. Here's a real-life case from the broad spectrum in between. In October 2012, while Superstorm Sandy was devastating the Northeast, @ComfortablySmug, a twenty-nine-year-old provocateur, irresponsibly alarmed millions by tweeting false information—that all major NYC subway lines were flooded, hence closed for the week; that Con Ed had stopped providing electricity to Lower Manhattan. Prompt Twitter responses by journalists and others with firsthand information outweighed the rumors, and panic was averted.

Admittedly, a natural disaster will

distract those immediately affected from all competing claims on their attention, freeing citizen journalists to monitor false information on social media and replace "bad information" with "good." However, the same phenomenon can be observed day to day on websites and in the letters columns of newspapers and magazines. Sometimes clues found in those sources require additional research, but for those who wish to be reliably informed, it's not too much to ask. ∎

ABOVE: **A fake Donald Trump tweet posted by a Chinese site that creates tweets to imitate the U.S. president. The tweets are then spread around social media, fooling many into thinking they're real**

EDU**CATION**

“ ”

Even one book, one pen, one child, and one teacher can change the world.

—MALALA YOUSAFZAI

TOP: **School walkouts protest frustration over standardized testing, 2015.**
LEFT: **Demonstrators outside of Tennessee's Education Summit protest Common Core education standards, 2014.**

FROM GRADE SCHOOL through grad school, students' work is assessed and rated. Simple report cards once sufficed for K-12; assessments were more complicated in college and graduate school but still comprehensible. Educators and governments began collecting statistics on the "results" of educational institutions in the nineteenth century. Education is about far more than grades, but because test scores are ubiquitous, grades and rankings of the institutions that award them frequently make the news.

The twenty-first century has produced divergent and often distressing ratings of individual schools, school systems, and schools of every country for which data are available. (Many small, less developed nations provide no data at all.) In the United States, free public K-12 education systems are also evaluated according to whether the schools are subject to district regulations, as has traditionally been the case, or are charter schools, which are exempt from such regulations but are accountable for their results, standing to lose their charters if performance is deemed inadequate.

In 2012 and 2016, the Social Progress Initiative of Deloitte, the big multinational professional services firm, published international education ratings. The first few countries in the 2016 list of the top twenty countries were South Korea, Japan, Singapore, Hong Kong, and Finland (number one in 2012). The UK, Canada, the Netherlands, Ireland, Poland, Denmark, Germany, and Russia follow. Number fourteen, the United States, spent 7.3 percent of its GDP on education in 2010, whereas higher-rated Finland, UK, Canada, Netherlands, Ireland, Poland, Germany, and Russia spent lower percentages. It's tempting to cast a large portion of blame for what appears to be less bang for the U.S. education buck on the expensive, controversial Common Core State Standards Initiative (CCSSI).

However, there are complicating factors. Common Core is a set of goals and expectations aimed at teaching students what they need to succeed in the new ball game called the twenty-first century. The initiative was designed to ensure consistency in the education of children whose families move from state to state, a sensible idea, given a highly mobile

population served by more than 4 million miles of roads. Another goal was to better prepare high school graduates to compete for jobs with people from countries having stronger educational systems. Finally, the CCSSI planners wanted to make available in every state courses that would give students a leg up in today's job market, which demands skills and knowledge on top of the traditional curricula.

Those worthy goals are sometimes achieved, but dissatisfaction with the program is high in many areas. A few states never participated; others have delayed implementing the standards or have dropped out by various means (repeal, rescission, opt-out). Florida, Massachusetts, and Minnesota are among the states that have modified Common Core tests to better match their own needs. Connecticut and Louisiana have delayed implementation.

Participation in the development of new tests has dropped dramatically. One reason for the total or partial rejection of Common Core is the observation of educators and parents in many states that having uniform standards

hasn't resulted in better accountability. However, it's worth pointing out that in setting up a system of national standards, size matters.

Of the top twenty countries in the Deloitte list, only Canada and Russia are bigger in geographical area than the United States. The other seventeen countries are considerably smaller. Whereas more than fifty U.S. states and territorial jurisdictions set their own educational policies, Canada has only ten provinces, each making its own rules. In the UK, the Scottish, Welsh, Northern Ireland, and English governments administer their respective education agendas. In Russia, the central government has much great authority over smaller political units than is true in the United States.

Smaller states—for example, Delaware and Vermont—are pleased with CCSSI. The District of Columbia, which implemented the standards quickly and at heavy cost, reports mixed results but remains committed to the program. However, almost everywhere else, the strong American traditions of states' rights and powerful local school boards have come into play as stakeholders realize that one size doesn't necessarily fit all.

With or without Common Core, highly variable requirements and many sets of local customs having nothing to do with education per se would be hard to reconcile. Differences in average per capita income from state to state and from region to region can mean differences in regional school budgets and resources, perceived school performance, perceived teacher performance, and the grades on students' report cards. And when students score poorly on Common Core exams, parents and teachers alike often blame the standardized tests. The economic pressure from the school boards to have students perform well often results in large amounts of time spent "teaching to the test." Yet this practice robs the same students of instruction in important areas not being tested, in addition to introducing and prolonging stress.

Always in the background of any discussion of education is the poverty factor. Hunger and disease often prevent children from taking advantage of even rudimentary learning opportunities. Children able to walk several miles in territory lacking paved roads may be little better off: their school may have no paper to write on and only a handful of tattered books to share. Many schools in impoverished areas are served by dedicated volunteers and the religious. However, in other cases children see only teachers who are unprepared for their task, or so indifferent to it that they're seldom present.

The children who emerge from under mosquito netting in the morning to trudge barefoot for miles in search of breakfast, if not an education, live in the Global South. Poverty elsewhere in the world is less dire, but it surely exists, in all the world's great capitals, as well as in rural areas. Steven Soderbergh, award-winning director of *Erin Brokovich*, offers the perspective of a parent who's neither a teacher nor an educrat: "There are three major social issues that [the United States] is struggling with: education, poverty, and drugs. Two of them we talk about, and one of them we don't."

Within our communities, it is key that as citizens we continue to work in support of local teachers. By keeping an eye—and casting our votes—at the district and state level, we can assist protests and walkouts, such as those that recently yielded victories in Oklahoma and Arizona in 2018, ensuring that our teachers have the support, funding, and power necessary to continue on their mission. ∎

"LET US THINK OF EDUCATION AS THE MEANS OF DEVELOPING OUR GREATEST ABILITIES, BECAUSE IN EACH OF US THERE IS A PRIVATE HOPE AND DREAM WHICH, FULFILLED, CAN BE TRANSLATED INTO BENEFIT FOR EVERYONE."
—JOHN F. KENNEDY

DEATH WITH DIGNITY

" "

The final disease that nature inflicts on us will determine the atmosphere in which we take our leave of life, but our own choices should be allowed, insofar as possible, to be the decisive factor in the manner of our going.

—DR. SHERWIN B. NULAND

BY SHARING THE story of her short, successful struggle to die with dignity, Brittany Maynard drew attention to a dilemma experienced by a growing number of individuals and their loved ones: what to do when a catastrophic medical diagnosis has only one possible ending, a lingering, painful death.

On New Year's Day, 2014, Maynard, age twenty-nine, learned that she had brain cancer. Radical surgery followed almost immediately, a partial craniotomy and a partial temporal lobe resection. By April, the tumor was back, more aggressive than before. Maynard's life expectancy was given as six months.

Maynard, her husband of just over a year, and other family members researched the only therapy on offer, full-brain radiation, which could perhaps have extended her life, but at the certain cost of a scalp covered with first-degree burns. The family discarded the hospice care option, since Maynard, who was otherwise healthy, might have remained alive while the cancer continued to attack her brain, robbing her of personality and cognitive skills, as her family watched helplessly.

Being mentally competent and possessing a prognosis of six months or less to live, Maynard was eligible for medical help in dying when the process itself became unbearable. The term for the result is "death with dignity," which can be achieved via assisted suicide. The final phases of a death with dignity are simple: the patient requests and receives from a physician a prescription for a lethal dose of a medication; at a time of the patient's choosing, he or she ends the dying process by self-ingesting the medication.

In the United States, early-stage seekers of assisted suicide face emotional, financial, and logistical nightmares unless their state authorizes the practice. Since California, where Maynard and her family lived, was a nonauthorizing state, she moved to Oregon, which was the first state to legalize assisted suicide. She had to establish residency, find a new home, get an Oregon driver's license, and change her voter registration. Her husband, Dan, took a leave of absence from his job. Shortly before she died,

Maynard wrote this:

> I've had the medication for weeks. I am not suicidal. If I were, I would have consumed that medication long ago. I do not want to die. But I am dying. And I want to die on my own terms.
>
> Having this choice at the end of my life has...given me a sense of peace during a tumultuous time that otherwise would be dominated by fear, uncertainty, and pain.
>
> Now, I'm able to move forward in my remaining days or weeks I have on this beautiful Earth, to seek joy and love and to spend time traveling to outdoor wonders of nature with those I love. And I know that I have a safety net.

On November 1, 2014, Brittany Maynard died peacefully, her loved ones at her side. On June 9, 2016, a death-with-dignity law went into effect in California. ■

TOP: **Right to die advocates gather outside the New Mexico Supreme Court, 2015.**
BOTTOM: **Debbie Ziegler, mother of Brittany Maynard, speaks to the media after the passage of death-with-dignity legislation, 2015.**

TOP: **Angela Davis, activist and outspoken opponent of the prison-industrial complex, addresses the Soviet International Women's Seminar in Moscow, 1972.**
BOTTOM: **Indian students outside of the U.S. Embassy in New Delhi, India, condemn U.S. imperialism and demand the release of Angela Davis, 1971.**

PRISON SYSTEMS

" "

Jails and prisons are designed to break human beings, to convert the population into specimens in a zoo—obedient to our keepers, but dangerous to each other.

—ANGELA DAVIS

BEFORE MOST OF the people working for prison reform today were born, the UN General Assembly adopted the International Covenant on Civil and Political Rights. This potentially valuable instrument, dated December 1966, has been in force since March 1976 as part of the International Bill of Human Rights. Enforcement is monitored by the UN Human Rights Committee, not to be confused with the UN Human Rights Counsel (formerly Human Rights Commission).

The covenant states that "all persons deprived of their liberty" are to receive humane treatment, consistent with respect for their inherent human dignity. Enforceability has been problematic.

The United States, claiming sovereign and other immunities, hasn't changed any laws to conform to the International Covenant on Civil and Political Rights (ICCPR), with the result that prisoners who believe their covenant-guaranteed rights are being violated can't sue in U.S. courts. Penologists representing South Asian states have cited such obstacles to compliance as prison overcrowding, difficulty in obtaining funding for improvements, and lack of cooperation from outside agencies and social welfare groups.

> "Neither slavery nor involuntary servitude, except as a punishment for crime whereof the party shall have been duly convicted, shall exist within the United States, or any place subject to their jurisdiction."
>
> —THE THIRTEENTH AMENDMENT TO THE UNITED STATES CONSTITUTION

All modern societies have at least one system of incarceration as well as levels of severity of inmate treatment. Weighted differently from system to system, even within a single administrative district, are three coexisting purposes of imprisonment itself. In the West, the oldest purpose—vengeance or retaliation—is usually disavowed unless a community seeks and heartily approves a harsh sentence for someone believed to be guilty of atrocities.

A purpose more defensible on humanitarian grounds, though not necessarily on grounds of effectiveness, is deterrence: "Lock 'em up! People will think twice about committing similar crimes, and those convicted once won't want to return to prison." That rationale loses some of its persuasiveness in the light of numbers of convictions for drug crimes, as well as high recidivism rates: 60 percent in the United States,

50 percent in the UK, according to a 2005 BBC report. The U.S. Sentencing Commission announced a slightly lower number (49.3 percent) in 2016 but pointed out that recidivism was much more likely among young offenders— those who went into prison with few legally marketable skills tend to come out with a prison record and little else.

A third approach combines punishment (incarceration) with programs aimed at "rehabilitation," a perhaps condescending term for giving individuals the opportunity to acquire the skills they need to function as law-abiding citizens. The skills may be as fundamental as reading or as psych-based as learning to delay gratification, with a variety of work and people skills in between. Where the will exists to fund and support a strong rehabilitation/retraining program, results have been encouraging. However, as the South Asian penologists found the

necessary will and budgetary leeway are often absent.

For the United States, which has the highest incarceration rate in the world, recent statistics are dismaying: with 5 percent of the world's population as of October 2015, the United States had 25 percent of the world's prisoners. Although scarcity and unreliability of data from authoritarian countries no doubt detracts from the accuracy of any global total, the U.S. contribution to that total, 2.5 million in 2015, is high by any standard.

Consistently paired with a high rate of incarceration is mistreatment of prisoners, which in turn is often said to be the product of overcrowding due to budgetary shortfalls that also preclude the hiring and training of sufficient correctional staff to maintain humane conditions. Nevertheless, reports of tragic deaths of prisoners cause shock waves in community after community,

as inmates of jails and prisons commit suicide or die because of failure of institutional controls or because cognitively impaired individuals were mistreated by inadequately supervised, often low-paid employees.

Withholding or delaying medical treatment of prisoners is also prevalent in overcrowded facilities. Those affected may be women in labor, prisoners dying of injuries inflicted by guards or other prisoners, or inmates in diabetic comas. Lifers and other long-term inmates who've developed chronic conditions may receive the least expensive meds, despite the availability of more effective drugs.

Inmates injured in the course of prison work assignments have had a better chance of being treated since the 1976 Supreme Court decision in *Estelle v. Gamble*. Badly hurt when a cotton bale fell on him in 1973, Texas prisoner J. W. Gamble got nowhere complaining of chest and back pains. He refused to work, was punished accordingly, and in 1974 submitted a handwritten complaint that led to Washington, DC. The Court didn't award Gamble damages; it did rule that in violation of the Eighth Amendment, he had received a "cruel and unusual punishment," namely, the failure of the prison to provide

appropriate care. As a result, Eighth Amendment protection became available to other U.S. prisoners—but for those laid low by illness or pain, availability alone may be meaningless.

However, numerous men and women often face injustice before day one in prison. Many inmates in the prime of life, especially minorities in the United States, have been incarcerated because mandatory sentencing guidelines prevented judges from making compassionate or commonsense exceptions. Others, talked into a guilty plea by an overburdened public defender, aren't guilty in the first place.

Most of these inmates have additional disadvantages as well: a background of poverty, education inadequate to meet their needs, and low or nonexistent funding for programs that could help them, to name a few.

The existence of a path from poverty to crime is universally acknowledged. Rendering that path unattractive or not the only option calls for either the abolition of poverty or the institution of a vast array of on-site opportunities for instruction, training, and growth, with support during parole.

Of course, not all crimes are committed by impoverished youth. Excesses of greed or passion lead to the downfall of a great number of educated, successful professionals, most of whom do their time and return to productive lives. The ability for such citizens to return to productive lives after doing time in prison further illustrates the imbalance of our current system. ■

RIGHT: **Activists in orange jumpsuits take part in a protest calling for the closure of Guantanamo Bay, 2016.**

The Power of Protest

"The Thirteenth Amendment to the United States Constitution did not end slavery... That amendment, which is still very much the law of the land today, as essential, historic, and groundbreaking as it was, has a poison pill, a trapdoor, an escape clause embedded in its core. With these three words, 'except as punishment,' the Thirteenth Amendment fell far short of offering the nation a full, complete, and true ban of the practice of slavery. Instead, the institution shape-shifted and morphed in peculiar ways—still primarily on black backs, but inside of less offensive systems and structures which made it a much more complicated and nebulous target."

—SHAUN KING

TOP: **Majory Stoneman Douglas student Emma Gonzalez holds a tearful moment of silence at the March for Our Lives rally.**
BOTTOM: **Cameron Kasky addresses fellow students as they rally in the countrywide school walkout.**
LEFT: **Over 800,000 protesters flood the streets of Washington, DC, during the March for Our Lives rally.**

GUN
CONTROL

"

To let these victims' lives be taken without any change
in return is an act of treason to our great country.

—LORENZO PRADO, PARKLAND SCHOOL SHOOTING SURVIVOR

ON APRIL 20, 1999, the Columbine massacre shifted the way America viewed gun control laws in relation to school shootings. Murdering twelve students and a teacher, in addition to injuring twenty-four others, Eric Harris and Dylan Klebold brought unheard of terror and attention to Jefferson County, Colorado, in executing the first major school shooting in our nation's history. While their true motives can never be explained, their attack sparked the national debates over gun control and conversations regarding bullying,

violence in video games, and violent communities brought together by the internet. Unfortunately, the Columbine massacre would also be the first of many large-scale school shootings across the nation.

In 2009, sociologist Ralph Larkin noted that the Columbine shooters "established a script" for subsequent school shootings. He specifically concluded that "Harris and Klebold committed their rampage shooting as an overtly political act in the name of oppressed students victimized by

> "We are going to be the kids you read about in textbooks. Not because we're going to be another statistic about mass shooting in America, but because...we are going to be the last mass shooting. Just like *Tinker v. Des Moines*, we are going to change the law."
>
> —EMMA GONZALEZ, PARKLAND SCHOOL SHOOTING SURVIVOR

their peers. Numerous post-Columbine rampage shooters referred directly to Columbine as their inspiration; others attempted to supersede the Columbine shootings in body count... The Columbine shootings redefined such acts not merely as revenge but as a means of protest of bullying, intimidation, social isolation, and public rituals of humiliation."

The students in schools today have grown up and experienced each day in a post-Columbine school system and society. Much as previous generations were trained to hide under desks in the face of nuclear war, students in schools today have been trained through drills and the apparent frequency in the media of these attacks to fear death by a school-shooter as a very real possibility.

Due to the climate created and the seeming lack of government response, the 208th school shooting since

Columbine is not the last school shooting to occur in the United States but thus far may be the most impactful in terms of protest and a shift in dialogue. On February 14th, 2018, nineteen-year-old Nicolas Jacob Cruz murdered seventeen teachers and classmates and injured countless others. However, unlike other school shootings post-Columbine, the students of Stoneman Douglas High School in Parkland, Florida, have made change their new mission.

Within days of the attack, students such as Cameron Kasky, Alex Wind, Emma Gonzalez, and David Hogg had made themselves household names, organizing the "Never Again" campaign and "March for Our Lives" protest, a nationwide march including a march on Washington in direct opposition to the current administration's response to the Parkland shooting. It quickly gained

additional support online not just from Parkland students but students and supporters nationwide. Celebrity support from Amal and George Clooney, Oprah Winfrey, Jeffrey Katzenberg, and Steven Spielberg brought millions of dollars to their campaign. On March 24, March for Our Lives had approximately 850,000 protesters in attendance in Washington with hundreds of thousands more protesting in over 850 cities globally. All fifty states had marches in support of their cause. With the goal of creating lasting change, protests continue to be scheduled throughout the nation as the students and others from "Generation Columbine" continue to be fed up with the National Rifle Association (NRA) and lax laws around gun control they support. Alternatively, counterprotests that also occurred in the wake of March for Our Lives continue to strive to

A demonstrator holds a sign protesting NRA funding at the March for Our Lives rally.

protect the threat firmer laws could pose to the second amendment. Rallying cries such as "Keep America Armed" and "Walk Up, Not Out" directly oppose what those in support of gun control are working to uphold.

As for the March for Our Lives organizers, many are touting what they pulled together as a revolution, "raw, authentic, and pure." The students and organizers had no corporate sponsorship signs, had no politicians or activists take the stage. Even with all the celebrities there to support, the only speakers at the event were students and youth in opposition of gun violence. Their age simply made their message more impactful. Parkland Students were not the only ones to speak, noting they wanted to ensure these messages were not only spoken by white voices. "We recognize that Parkland received more attention because of its affluence," Jaclyn Corin, a survivor of the Parkland shooting, said in her speech. "But we share this stage today and forever with those communities who have always stared down the barrel of a gun."

Dr. Martin Luther King Jr.'s granddaughter, nine-year-old Yolanda Renee King, told the crowd she dreams of a "gun-free world, period."

Eleven-year-old Naomi Wadler took the stage, stating she was on stage to represent "African American girls whose stories don't make the front page of every national newspaper."

"I represent the African American women who are victims of gun violence, who are simply statistics, instead of vibrant, beautiful girls full of potential," she continued.

Despite the impact of March for Our Lives, the conversation around gun control continues to wage. Hope continues to spark for change, even as attacks in schools and against the public continue to occur. As Emma Gonzalez said in response to those first attacks, "[I] noticed...when you mentioned the Declaration of Independence you talked a lot about liberties and the pursuit of happiness, but never about life. Do we not deserve the right to live anymore? Can we take this as a Protect-Guns-not-Students message?" ■

LEFT: **Majory Stoneman Douglas students and other young victims of gun violence stand together on stage at the end of the March for Our Lives rally.**

"

We've had enough of thoughts and prayers... To every lawmaker out there: No longer can you take money from the NRA. No longer can you fly under the radar doing whatever it is that you want to do... We are coming after every single one of you and demanding that you take action.

—DELANEY TARR, PARKLAND SCHOOL SHOOTING SURVIVOR

CONCLUSION: HOW CAN **YOU** CHANGE THE WORLD?

RESEARCH • SPEAK OUT • VOLUNTEER
TALK • LISTEN • DONATE • MARCH • VOTE
CALL YOUR LOCAL REPRESENTATIVES
START YOUR OWN ORGANIZATION!

HOW CAN YOU change the world? There's one simple, irrefutable answer: slowly and stubbornly. For centuries people of goodwill have fought for the rights of others: an enslaved and subsequently oppressed minority, workers, and women, whose rights are often violated in multiple spheres (the buzzword is *intersectionality*). More recently, but reflecting long-festering injustices, the rights of other ethnic and cultural minorities—immigrants and their descendants, the LGBT community—have been drawing vigorous, well-deserved support.

In the West, much progress has been made; in many less developed areas, progress has been remarkable but still insufficient; in countries that are utterly impoverished or governed by highly authoritarian rulers, there's been backsliding, evidenced by starvation and short life spans on the one hand, and by torture, long imprisonments, and summary executions on the other.

The seeming intractability of problems in some areas by no means prevents individuals from working for change in others. "If not now, when? If not me, who?" is a good starting point. Also important: "There's strength in numbers."

Precisely because of the strength in numbers, "volunteer" is high on anyone's list of answers to the central question. A volunteer group can be global in scope like Amnesty International, or small and nameless, like people you may see policing neighborhood roads to pick up cans, bottles, and bags of dog poop. You don't need a cause-emblazoned T-shirt, but it doesn't hurt to wear a discreet wristband or two identifying you as a supporter of causes you believe in.

Volunteer groups are a good first choice because they already have some structure and may offer training. In addition, you'll have the company of more experienced volunteers and the benefit of planning by a coordinating committee. There'll also be knowledgeable people to do the bureaucratic heavy lifting. That is, it won't be on a newbie to get parade permits or arrange for parking and sanitation at a big outdoor event, unless, of course, you have the requisite experience with your city and with outside contractors.

Volunteer groups are also easy to find. They're as close as your browser, as close as the bulletin board in a laundromat or feed store you visit often. High schools and colleges also make information about volunteer opportunities accessible. Or just wait. A friend who shares your concerns will ask you for help in an organized protest or ongoing campaign.

Vying with "Volunteer" for most frequent answer to "How can you change the world?" is "Send money." However, since no one with an internet account or mail service can avoid requests for donations, it's necessary to pick and choose. Many prefer to avoid the big, ultrarespectable disaster relief and worldwide antipoverty organizations on the grounds that they're well supported by deep-pockets parties, and thus one person's relatively small contribution to a less well known charity or aid group would have more effect.

There's something to be said for the choice to skip the most visible relief agencies, but you still need to determine which organizations are the most worthy of your support. An excellent resource is Charity Navigator (charitynavigator.org), an independent evaluator of the financial health and transparency of thousands of U.S. charitable organizations. Charity Navigator may tell you more than you want to know. On the other hand, you may be surprised to learn than one animal welfare group spends a huge percentage of its money on fund-raising and administrative costs, whereas another is chaired by someone whose annual salary is $18,000. Your browser will show other websites that rate charities.

Local charities, civic organizations, and houses of worship publicize their initiatives and make it easy to volunteer for or contribute to those that intrigue or compel you. Large international organizations also offer opportunities to help people all over the world achieve sustainable self-sufficiency while conserving natural resources and promoting strong communities. Some well-known organizations will accept a contribution in the low two figures and pool it with other donations to buy an expensive item (a heifer, say, or a village water pump: heifer.org); others will pass along as a microloan a similar amount that will enable someone in a poverty-stricken area to accumulate enough inventory or equipment to start a small business (kiva.org).

Volunteering, often or occasionally, and donating, whether you give until it hurts to a cause you're passionate about or agree to add a dollar or two to your grocery bill for the Special Olympics or the March of Dimes, aren't the only ways to "change the world." In addition to putting effort into volunteer work or contributing money to nonprofits, you can help people and the planet by focusing inward. This isn't a finger-wagging proscription, as in "Don't make so many frivolous purchases" or "Don't fritter away so much time on video games." It's an invitation to consider the ramifications of how you, a kind, environmentally conscious person, might amplify the effects of the good things you're already doing.

For example, no matter how rigorously you recycle, the items you're discarding and the replacements you'll buy came from somewhere. The U.S. Department of Labor maintains an eye-opening list of countries that use child labor and forced labor, including the classes of items so produced (dol.gov/ilab/reports/child-labor/list-of-goods). So it's worthwhile to look into practices in garment making that you want to discourage. Then, after you've done your research, tell your friends, family members, and perhaps a friendly clerk at a favorite store who could influence future purchases. Contact a senator or congressional representative with a specialty in trade to share your findings and see how you might be able to help.

Other means of bringing about positive change begin even closer to home. The smallest action—a smile at anyone at all, a "Take your time" to a harried server, any random act of kindness—can give a lift to those you encounter. Pay it forward; follow one simple grace with another, and another. A serene vibe, conveying acceptance and nonjudgmentalism, can be your biggest weapon in the fight to right the world's wrongs. ∎